Smoothie Recipe Book

Slim Smoothies

Healthy & Nutritious Low Calorie Smoothie Recipes for Weight Loss, Improved Health, and Happiness

By: *Diana Clayton*

Table of Contents

Cleanse and Detox Smoothies 57

Brain Boosting Smoothies 71

Introduction

If you don't already drink smoothies - you should start. Today! There is no easier way to inject a boost of goodness into your body and nourish yourself from the inside out. Smoothies don't just look pretty and taste great, they are absolutely incredible for you too. Boasting an impressive list of health benefits, their inclusion in your diet is something that can no longer be over looked.

Recent research has revealed some interesting facts about vegetables. While we all know the importance of getting enough fruits and veggies in our diet, did you know that cooking certain vegetables, like broccoli for instance, renders many of the compounds in it useless and completely negates some of the health benefits? Nope? Don't feel alone, I didn't either! So then I figured chewing on some raw broccoli would be the way to go? Well I was wrong again! Scientists have highlighted that chewing raw vegetables is not always best either. The individual cells that make up the vegetable in question is where all the vitamins and minerals reside. When we chew, some but not all of those cells burst, so only some of the nutrition is released into our body.

So what's the best way to eat veggies then if you can't cook them and can't eat them raw? The answer is simple - smoothies!

Smoothies are often referred to as "pure nutrition". This is because it has been proven over and over that pulverizing your fruits and veggies in a blender breaks them down at a cellular level. All the cell walls are demolished and that means ALL the nutrition is released! In their liquid state they are primed for absorption by the body and this process begins in the mouth. Digestion is so much easier as the goodness is just waiting to be sucked up by your body. No more will your body have to work so hard to digest whole bits of roughly chewed food to extract only a fraction of the nutrition. If you are smart, just one smoothie a day can meet all your fruit and vegetable requirements in the most high quality form.

Smoothies vs. Juicing:

Now I think here is a good place to differentiate between smoothies and juicing. The practice of juicing, whereby you extract the juice from fresh fruits and vegetables, has become quite popular in recent years and while I am not saying it is not a healthier option than store bought juices (it is 100% natural after all), it is not always the best option in terms of health or nutrition. You see, when you juice you discard all the pulp and that is nothing short of nutrition sacrilege! The pulp not only contains a ton of nutrition that you are literally just throwing into the garbage can, but it is where one all important substance can be found - fiber! Fiber is vital for a healthy functioning digestive system. Not only does it help to keep

1

you regular, but it binds to harmful toxins in the gut and helps the body to eliminate them. Even more noteworthy, smoothies can actually replace a full meal since they help to keep you feeling nice and full. Juices on the other hand are often as calorie-dense as a smoothie, but leave you hungry and unsatisfied. So by all means enjoy fresh juices, but make it a rule to never replace a smoothie with juice – a smoothie will be more satisfying, every time.

How to ensure top class smoothies – choosing quality equipment and ingredients:

Now just as if you had to use poor quality ingredients while baking, your cake would flop, a smoothie can only be as good as what you put into it. Never ever buy inferior quality produce. Always try to get the freshest fruit and vegetables that you can and where possible go organic! Your local farmers market will be the best place to get super fresh produce that is organically grown at a fraction of the cost you would pay for the same thing in the grocery store. Because the goods sold at places like this are not grown for commercial distribution, they are far more likely to be grown sans the harsh chemicals and pesticides that are used in larger scale farming practices. When you use delicious fresh juicy ingredients, your smoothies will be bursting with flavor and will have you hooked after a few sips.

Even if you have the best quality ingredients on the planet, you are not likely to have a positive smoothie experience if you have an unreliable blender. I cannot stress this enough - this is one area where you do not want to be thrifty! Yes, getting a good blender could cost a bit initially, but it will pay for itself for years to come. Getting a cheap, run of the mill blender is just going to mean you are going to be replacing it a few months down the line when the motor burns out or when you are choking on whole bits of fruit and vegetables that haven't been blitzed properly. Trust me, there is nothing worse than getting hard bits of skin or fibers in your mouth first thing in the morning or having to jump up from the table 10 times to rinse and unclog your straw. If smoothies are to become part of your life, you need to make up your mind to invest in a decent blender, because what you really are doing is making a crucial commitment to your body and to your good health - and that my friend, is priceless!

Now let's get down to the nitty gritty facts of performance and mechanics. What should you be looking for in this piece of kitchen equipment? You need a blender with a good motor – that is not negotiable. One that is durable, powerful and is not going to burn out while screeching and groaning to get your veggies liquidized. Some blenders come with a built in cooling fan which stops the motor from overheating at high speeds. If you can find one with this fail safe it is preferable. You need a blender that is versatile. It's a good idea to, try to find one that is multi-functional and can blend, chop, churn, mix, pulverize and liquidize all in one – this makes parting with that cash a little easier. Now as your regular Joe soap on the street is no engineer, make sure you find a blender that is easy to use. There is nothing more disheartening than getting home with your new purchase proudly under your arm, only to open the box and spend the next three hours trying to figure out what all the buttons do! You need a blender that is tough, with strong, sharp blades that are not going to rust. Those blades need to be able to tear through anything from a banana to ice cubes and everything in between. It should be built to handle biggish pieces too so you don't have to spend ages peeling and chopping. And it needs to be able to liquidize everything fairly quickly. A smoothie should not take you longer than about 5 minutes to make – they are supposed to embody simplicity and make it easier for you to consume your fruit and vegetables. So shop around and compare prices and brands before making your final decision and be sure you've done your research before making your purchase. Lastly, please make sure your brand offers a warranty! Most good, reliable brands will offer some kind of warranty for repairs.

<u>Tips and tricks to blend the perfect smoothie EVERY time:</u>

Right so you have invested in an incredible blender, you have been to your local farmers market and have a stash of fresh produce scattered across your kitchen counter - now you are wondering how to bring it all together into an amazing smoothie. The perfect smoothie is nothing short of art - trying to get the perfect blend of ingredients that delights the taste buds with a not too thick, not too thin consistency can be a daunting prospect for beginner smoothie makers. But fortunately like art, smoothies are a subjective experience and depend largely on your personal tastes and individual preferences. That is not to say that there aren't a few universal tips and tricks that will help you blend the perfect smoothie time and again. Firstly remember to have fun. Experiment with a whole lot of different combinations. Keep a record of what you like and chalk up the ones you don't to experience. That being said, smoothies are incredibly forgiving and very easy to "fix". If it's a little too thick, add a little liquid to balance the texture. Not sweet enough, add a little honey or a date or two. Dates are THE most incredible natural sweeteners and completely overlooked most of the time. If you have braved one of those green smoothies that are all the rage at the moment and its tasting a little like your weekly pile of lawn clippings, simply add some tropical fruit to mask the flavor.

Building a smoothie has a couple of staple steps and from there on out you have free creative reign. Firstly, your smoothie needs a liquid of some kind to get those veggies and fruits going in the blender. While water is an incredibly healthy option, it does tend to dilute the flavor somewhat. Some awesome and really tasty options are things like coconut water and green tea for the very health conscious. For those with a more relaxed outlook, you can throw in some fruit juices (freshly squeezed of course), skim milk or for an added flavor dimension for those who are not partial or intolerant towards dairy products, try one of the nut milks. Then you need your chosen fruits and vegetables. Bananas, apples, pears and the like are the smoothie staples that you include in most recipes, but then try to find a more exotic ingredient to jazz things up a bit like kiwi fruit or papaya. Berries are always a great inclusion, not only for their incredible taste but the health benefits they offer are unparalleled. If you are adding veggies too, spinach and kale are good starter ones. This is because their mild flavor is easily hidden beneath the other tastes and you won't even know they are there while still reaping all the goodness. Then you need your piece de resistance so to speak – that special ingredient that adds a little something extra. Nuts, seeds, oats, spices like cinnamon or nutmeg, fresh herbs or even a splash of vanilla extract all add that bit of pizzazz and fancy up an otherwise drab smoothie. Now in terms of add on ingredients the lists are literally endless and most often they tend to fall into the category of superfoods –

those more exotic ingredients for special occasions. At the start of every chapter I have included a list of extra ingredients that can be added to your basic smoothie recipes depending on what health aspect is your focus.

Once you have your basic ingredients outlined, you are going to need to focus on texture. Smoothie texture is EVERYTHING! You do not want gritty bits in your mouth or pieces of spinach in your teeth. Too watery makes things very bland and too thick is going to require a spoon rather than a straw to consume it! No matter what ingredients you have chosen, everything needs to be completely smooth – it's right there in the title – SMOOTHies! Your chosen blender will go a long way towards achieving this, but you will also need a filler ingredient. Something that binds the rest together in a delicious creamy blend of goodness. Cream is OUT and yes that means ice cream too folks – we are focusing on health here remember! The absolute best thing for thickening up your smoothie is to freeze some of your fruits beforehand. Make sure you freeze them fresh and don't allow them to thaw too much before adding them to your blender. Two of the best frozen fruits to add are grapes and berries. They are small enough that most blenders will handle them frozen and they blitz up quickly adding a lovely slushy, icy texture that finishes off your smoothie to perfection. If this is not your thing, but you still like a thicker, creamier smoothie, then what I propose is things like yoghurt, avocados, coconut oil, coconut cream (whipped if you like for extra creamy thickness) and nut butters. These are exquisite elegance at their finest and add such an amazing quality to your smoothie that you will never look back! If you are going for yoghurt, plain, fat free Greek is best in terms of health. Try to avoid the flavored yoghurts as they are packed full of artificial colorants and flavors and a ton of sugar. If you have a sweet tooth and the natural sweetness of the fruit is not enough for you, you can sweeten your smoothie but stick to natural sources of sweetness. I have already mentioned that dates are an excellent option. Other great options are honey, maple syrup, and stevia. (Check the ingredients to ensure your stevia is all natural). Remember to use these sparingly. You want to get to a point where you no longer need additional sweetness and all your sugar comes from the fruit.

And that's it! – It really is that easy to have delicious smoothies in your life absolutely every day. What follows are 81 absolutely amazing & nutritious low calorie smoothie recipes to get you started on your journey towards health, wellness, and vitality.

For your convenience, all smoothies are divided up into different sections according to the primary area of health they focus on. Please note that although there is a section for "Super Weight Loss Smoothies" **all** of the smoothies in this book are low in calories. The "Super Weight Loss" section simply contains recipes with ingredients that give weight loss efforts an even greater boost! So feel free to enjoy *all* of the incredible smoothies that follow! Don't allow any particular category to restrict you. Just because maybe you're not looking for anti-aging smoothies doesn't mean that you won't love them! The categories are simply there to guide you, but ultimately **all** of the smoothies are delicious and *amazing* for your well-being. So what are you waiting for? Get into the kitchen and start experimenting.

Happy blending!
- Diana

Immune Support Smoothies

Where most people fall short is when they treat immune boosting as a seasonal activity. Right before winter everyone loads up on Vitamin C and takes all kinds of supplements to boost their immunity and ward off the germs that cause illness. What most people don't realize is that if immune support became part of your regular routine, there would be no need to try boost your immunity seasonally and sickness would become a thing of the past. Building up and keeping your immune system in peak condition is what will keep the germs at bay rather than the ebb and flow of bombarding your body with vitamins when it's cold and then slacking off as the weather warms.

Ideally, your immune system should work like a well-oiled machine, enhancing your body and fighting off germs – naturally. A diesel car is not going to run properly on regular fuel and similarly if you do not give your body the right raw materials, it too is going to chug along before breaking down. Keeping your body healthy should not be a chore and that is where smoothies come in. There is no quicker or simpler way to load your body full of all the goodness, vitamins and minerals it needs to stay healthy all year long. The longer your immune system stays strong and healthy, the more resilient and capable it will be.

So what are the right foods to include in your smoothies to keep your cellular army fighting fit? A good place to start is with foods that are high in Vitamin C, like apples, berries, citrus fruits, papaya, kiwi fruit, cantaloupe, grapefruit, and leafy greens. These kinds of common ingredients should form the basis of your immune boosting smoothies because they provide your body with a healthy whack of disease fighting vitamins and minerals.

BUT…Every army needs a specially trained task force and for our body, this comes in the form of superfoods. While the smoothies in the recipes below will do their part to boost your immune system, if you are able to get your hands on some of these amazing 'extras', include them in any one of these smoothies for an additional kick of potent immune boosting power. The best immune boosting superfoods for smoothies are: ginger, garlic, turmeric, ashwaganda (herb), astragalus (Chinese herb), hemp seeds, Echinacea, coconut oil, kefir, oats, barley, green tea, kombucha (Asian tea known as the "immortal health elixir"), apple cider vinegar, camu camu berry, acai berries (or the frozen acai pulp), goji berries, spirulina, honey and bee pollen. Most of these ingredients can be found at your local health store and are easily incorporated into your basic smoothie recipes.

So without further ado, here are some immune boosting smoothies that will not only knock your socks off, but knock those disease causing bugs for a six! Enjoy!

Peaches and "Cream" Smoothie

Rev up your immune system with this vitamin enriched fruity smoothie. Fresh ginger provides not only deliciously fragrant undertones and adds depth to an otherwise bland smoothie, but also provides the critical disease fighting component. The citrus adds an extra flavor dimension as well as packing a big Vitamin C punch to help fight off unwanted germs and restore good health.

Yields: 2 Servings

Ingredients:

- 2 peaches, chopped
- 270ml fat free Greek yoghurt
- 120ml orange juice – freshly squeezed
- 2 tablespoons lemon juice
- 1 tablespoon honey (optional)
- ½ teaspoon fresh ginger – minced
- ¼ teaspoon cinnamon

Directions:

1. Add all the ingredients to your blender and blend until smooth.
2. Serve chilled.

Health Benefits:

- ✓ Disease fighting
- ✓ Immune boosting
- ✓ Vitamin enriched for overall health and vitality
- ✓ Cholesterol free
- ✓ Very low in sodium
- ✓ High in Vitamin C and B6

Nutritional values per serving: Calories: 176; Total Fat: .8g; Cholesterol: 0mg; Sodium: 4mg; Potassium: 342mg; Carbohydrates: 31.8g; Protein: 11.8g

Easy Peezy Pomegranate Smoothie!

This simple 3 ingredient smoothie is packed full of antioxidants. It is quick and easy to make and therefore perfect for those on the go people whose immune systems are under pressure from lifestyle stress. Also a great smoothie for those who work-out, to restore and replenish the body.

Yields: 2 Servings

Ingredients:

- 540ml fat free Greek yoghurt
- 225g frozen raspberries
- 360ml pomegranate juice
- stevia to taste (optional)

Directions:

1. Add all the ingredients to your blender and blend until smooth.
2. Drink it up…. Easy Peezy!

Health benefits:

- ✓ High in Vitamin C
- ✓ Good source of protein
- ✓ High in fiber
- ✓ Low in saturated fat

- ✓ Cholesterol Free!
- ✓ Low in sodium
- ✓ Good source of potassium

Nutritional values per serving: Calories: 196; Total Fat: 0.8g; Cholesterol: 0mg; Sodium: 7mg; Potassium: 714mg; Carbohydrates: 47.3g; Protein: 21g

Simply Scrumptious Summer Smoothie

This smoothie is great for summer! The watermelon makes it a refreshing and thirst quenching drink to enjoy at any time of the day. Lycopene in the watermelon inhibits inflammation which combined with its antioxidant properties is great for healing. Aloe Vera is thought to stimulate white blood cell production which helps our immune systems fight viruses. And it tastes fantastic to boot!

Yields: 1 Serving

Ingredients:

- 760g frozen watermelon
- 270ml fat free Greek yoghurt
- ½ fresh cucumber
- 1 tablespoon chopped fresh mint
- 1 tablespoon Aloe Vera juice (optional)
- Water as needed

Directions:

1. Add all the ingredients to your blender and blend until smooth.
2. Serve chilled over crushed ice.
3. Enjoy!

Health benefits:

- ✓ Very high in vitamin C
- ✓ Very high in vitamin A
- ✓ Very high in vitamin B6
- ✓ High in potassium
- ✓ High in magnesium
- ✓ High in iron
- ✓ Low in fat, cholesterol and sodium

Nutritional values per serving: Calories: 52; Total Fat: 0.3g; Cholesterol: 0mg; Sodium: 4mg; Potassium: 235mg; Carbohydrates: 12.3g; Protein: 11.3g

Tropical Bite Smoothie

Tropical Bite Smoothie

Tropical fruits and green veggies with a bite of cayenne - Yum! It is high in antioxidants and full of fatty acids in just the right ratio. The Capsaicin from the cayenne pepper is known to increase metabolism, lower blood pressure and have cancer inhibiting properties.

Yields: 2 Servings

Ingredients:

- 100g blueberries
- 1 handful of baby spinach
- ½ an avocado, pitted and peeled
- ½ banana
- 1 tablespoon raw cacao powder
- 1 tablespoon raw honey
- Pinch of cayenne
- 360ml water
- Handful of ice blocks

Directions:

1. Place the blueberries, avocado, banana, and spinach in your blender. Now pour in half the water and blitz for a few seconds.
2. Add the pinch of cayenne and the honey.
3. Keep blitzing while adding water until the desired consistency is reached.
4. Add the ice blocks and blitz once more.
5. Drink immediately while cold. Yummmmmy!

Health Benefits:

- ✓ Immune boosting
- ✓ Disease fighting
- ✓ High in Vitamin C and B6
- ✓ High in Omega 3 and 6
- ✓ Rich in fiber
- ✓ High in Potassium
- ✓ Cholesterol Free!
- ✓ Low in Sodium

Nutritional values per serving: Calories: 161; Total Fat: 7.6g; Cholesterol: 0mg; Sodium: 16mg; Potassium: 430mg; Carbohydrates: 25.6g; Protein: 2.0g

Green Machine Smoothie

Avocado is a great source of high quality fatty acids and is also known to help reduce inflammation. Green tea and spinach are loaded with antioxidants which will boost your immune system. Green tea is also known to boost your metabolism thus aiding in weight loss. Ginger and cinnamon also have anti-inflammatory properties with cinnamon also boosting insulin sensitivity. One Green Machine Smoothie!!

Yields: 1 Serving

Ingredients:

- 200ml chilled green tea
- 1 apple, chopped and cored
- ½ an avocado – pitted and peeled
- 1 handful of baby spinach
- 1 teaspoon cinnamon
- 1 teaspoon fresh ginger – minced

Directions:

1. Make a pot of green tea and keep it chilled in the refrigerator.
2. Add the ingredients in the correct quantities to your blender.
3. Blend until smooth and keep chilled until you consume.
4. Drink and feel healthier!

Health benefits:

- ✓ High in good fatty acids
- ✓ Anti-inflammatory qualities to aid immune system
- ✓ Helps to regulate blood sugar
- ✓ Cholesterol Free!
- ✓ Low in sodium and sugar
- ✓ High in dietary fiber
- ✓ High in Vitamins A and C

Nutritional values per serving: Calories: 220; Total Fat: 19.8g; Cholesterol: 0mg; Sodium: 39mg; Potassium: 605mg; Carbohydrates: 12.3g; Protein: 2.6g

Power Punch Smoothie

This smoothie packs a powerful punch of vitamins! There are carrots for beta-carotene - this antioxidant is known for its anti-cancer properties. Orange is well known for its vitamin C and is associated with lowering the risk of colon cancer and its immune boosting properties. Blueberries are packed full of antioxidants and phytochemicals. These help to slow the rate of memory decline and protect the heart. The flax seed gives a healthy dose of omega-3 fatty acids.

Yields: 1 Serving

Ingredients:

- ½ banana
- ½ whole carrot
- 3 strawberries
- 180ml fresh orange juice
- 1 handful of baby spinach
- 1 tablespoon blueberries
- 1 teaspoon flax seed

Directions:

1. Add the orange juice and the carrot to your blender and blitz until the carrot is properly chopped.
2. Add the rest of the ingredients and blend until smooth.
3. Drink and enjoy!

Health benefits:

- ✓ High in vitamins A, B6 and C
- ✓ Omega-3 fatty acids
- ✓ Cholesterol Free!
- ✓ Very low in saturated fats
- ✓ Low in sodium
- ✓ High in potassium

Nutritional values per serving: Calories: 178; Total Fat: 1.3g; Cholesterol: 0mg; Sodium: 36mg; Potassium: 827mg; Carbohydrates: 40.2g; Protein: 3.2g

Caribbean Delight Smoothie

Pineapples contain bromelain which helps digestion and are also thought to have anti-inflammatory properties. Coconut milk adds the flavors of the islands and is good for the heart and boosts the immune system along with pawpaw. As an added plus coconut milk has been shown to be an effective aid to weight loss. Chia seeds are the secret ingredient, not only binding it all together but they pull their weight by improving the fatty acid omega-3 to omega-6 ratio and helping to stabilize blood sugar.

Yields: 2 Servings

Ingredients:

- 280g fresh or frozen pineapple
- ½ large papaya, chopped & seeds removed
- 300ml coconut milk
- 1 tablespoon chia seeds

Directions:

1. Add all the ingredients to your blender and blitz until smooth.
2. Sip slowly and dream of the islands!

Health benefits:

- ✓ Anti-inflammatory agents helps immune system
- ✓ Omega-3 fatty acids
- ✓ Cholesterol Free!
- ✓ Low in sodium
- ✓ Very high in Vitamin C and manganese

Nutritional values per serving: Calories: 418; Total Fat: 31.5g; Cholesterol: 0mg; Sodium: 56mg; Potassium: 730mg; Carbohydrates: 34.9g; Protein: 5.5g

Apple Salad Smoothie

Kale is one of the best sources of dietary iron. Celery contains many anti-cancer properties and is also very low in calories. Lime and lemon juices offer healthy doses of vitamin C along with antibiotic and antioxidant effects. Apples contain pectin an important prebiotic as well as quercetin which has been found to have anti-inflammatory and antioxidant boosting properties. The coconut water will help to replenish electrolytes. Mix it all together and you have a smoothie that is designed to boost our immune system's ability to fight infections. Here's to your good health!

Yields: 1 Serving

Ingredients:

- 1 handful of kale
- 1 red apple cored – skin on
- ½ stalk celery
- 60ml lime juice
- 60ml lemon juice
- Coconut water as needed

Directions:

1. Add all the ingredients to your blender and blitz.
2. Add coconut water and blend until the smoothie reaches the desired consistency.
3. Drink it up... Cheers!

Health benefits:

- ✓ High iron content
- ✓ Good source of antioxidants
- ✓ Anti-inflammatory properties
- ✓ Cholesterol Free!

- ✓ Very low in saturated fats
- ✓ High in fiber, manganese and potassium
- ✓ Very high in A, B6 and C

Nutritional values per serving: Calories: 166; Total Fat: 0.7g; Cholesterol: 0mg; Sodium: 36mg; Potassium: 682mg; Carbohydrates: 37.4g; Protein: 2.1g

Chocolate Banana Splash Smoothie

Bananas are easily digestible and a great source of potassium which is essential for heart health. Almonds enhance the immune system by inhibiting free radicals and are a source of prebiotics, which promote healthy bacteria in the gut. Oats are high in fiber and have also been found to contain beta glucans which can boost our defense against bacteria and viruses. Honey is full of antioxidants, antiviral and antibacterial goodness. This is a deliciously essential supplement for flu season.

Yields: 1 Serving

Ingredients:

- 1 frozen banana
- 270ml unsweetened almond milk
- 1 tablespoon raw cacao powder
- 1 tablespoon raw honey
- 2 tablespoons virgin coconut oil
- 1 teaspoon cinnamon

Directions:

1. Blitz the banana and the almond milk in your blender.
2. Add the rest of the ingredients and blend until smooth.
3. Drink and be healthy.

Health benefits:

- ✓ High in calcium
- ✓ Contains free radical inhibitors
- ✓ Prebiotic qualities
- ✓ High in Vitamin E
- ✓ Antibacterial, antiviral and antioxidant
- ✓ Cholesterol Free!
- ✓ Very low in sodium

Nutritional values per serving: Calories: 232; Total Fat: 15.6g; Cholesterol: 0mg; Sodium: 93mg; Potassium: 307mg; Carbohydrates: 25.4g; Protein: 1.9g

Beauty, Anti-aging and Radiant Skin Smoothies

The quest for beauty and the fountain of youth is something that dominates modern society and unfortunately, beauty seems to be equated with youth. Our burgeoning plastic surgery industry is testimony to just how many people are desperate to turn back the hands of time and to the importance people place on external appearance. Aging is one of the huge existential crises facing humans and despite our best intentions to age gracefully, I think we would all welcome a magic potion to halt the visible signs of aging.

We all make an effort to look our best on the outside but what many fail to realize is that true beauty actually comes from within. When I say this, I am not meaning to refer to the adage that it's our personality that counts when it comes to labelling someone as beautiful, I literally mean, that to look good on the outside we need to nourish ourselves from the inside. Aging is caused at a cellular level by free radical damage. Free radicals enter our systems from the foods we ingest and from some environmental stresses such as sun damage. Alcohol, smoking and the unhealthy chemical additives in our modern diet are also some of the biggest culprits. Antioxidants from the healthy foods we ingest are able to bind with free radicals and 'defuse' them, thereby stopping them from causing further cellular damage.

Someone who lives a "fast" lifestyle indulging in fast foods, alcohol, smoking and the like can never show the outer effects of beauty when the inside of them has been poisoned. Eating healthy food, drinking lots of water, and exercise are the inner hallmarks of outer beauty. We need to make sure that we are perfect at a cellular level, before we can display that beauty for the world to see.

Now I am not claiming to hold the elixir of youth and I am not going to make false promises. What I am going to do is show you what ingredients to include in your smoothies that have been proven effective in slowing down the visible signs of aging, leaving you looking more radiant and youthful than ever before. In accordance with the above, you need to load up on antioxidant rich foods and there is no greater source than berries. In addition to your regular blueberries, strawberries and raspberries, try some blackberries, cranberries, goji berries and acai berries for something different. Other foods that tip the antioxidant scale favorably are cacao powder, pomegranates, black plums, pecan nuts, apples, pears and cinnamon. Add any one of these to your smoothies to rev up the antioxidant level and stop visible aging in its tracks!

Berries Galore Smoothie

This smoothie will definitely kick-start your day! With 3 different kinds of berries and antioxidant rich pomegranate juice this smoothie will blast the free radicals in your body that cause aging. As an added bonus the potassium in the banana will keep your heart healthy and functioning well.

Yields: 2 Servings

Ingredients:

- 45g strawberries
- 30g raspberries
- 45g blueberries
- 120ml apple juice
- ½ banana
- few ice cubes

Directions:

1. Blend the ice, and the apple juice first until the ice is completely broken up.
2. Add the rest of the ingredients and blend until smooth.
3. Drink and feel youthful!

Health benefits:

- ✓ Very high in vitamin C and B6
- ✓ High in manganese
- ✓ High in dietary fiber
- ✓ Rich in antioxidants

- ✓ Very low sodium
- ✓ Very low in saturated fat
- ✓ Cholesterol Free!
- ✓ Heart healthy

Nutritional values per serving: Calories: 80; Total Fat: 0.2g; Cholesterol: 0mg; Sodium: 7mg; Potassium: 244mg; Carbohydrates: 19.3g; Protein: 0.8g

Raspberry Rage Smoothie

This delicious smoothie does all the right things, it contains the antioxidants needed to fight free radicals and has all the vitamins to boost your immune system and give you a healthy glow. All this and it is low in calories too!

Yields: 2 Servings

Ingredients:

- 130g raspberries
- 75g blackberries
- 75g strawberries
- ½ pear – cored
- 120ml water

Directions:

1. Blend all the ingredients together until smooth, adding water until the desired consistency is reached.
2. Relax and let the smoothie work its magic from within.

Health benefits:

- ✓ Very high in vitamin C and B6
- ✓ Very high in manganese
- ✓ Very high in dietary fiber
- ✓ Very low in sodium
- ✓ Very low in saturated fat
- ✓ Cholesterol Free!

Nutritional values per serving: Calories: 79; Total Fat: 0.8g; Cholesterol: 0mg; Sodium: 2mg; Potassium: 248mg; Carbohydrates: 18.9g; Protein: 1.6g

Coconut Cream Smoothie

Coconut oil contains healthy fats and vitamins that are crucial for a healthy skin. Including just a tablespoon packs this smoothie full of vitamin E which aids skin growth, rejuvenation, and repair and also contains lauric acid which is an anti-microbial. The saturated fat in the oil is also known to protect skin from UV damage. If you'd like a stronger coconut taste, replace the almond milk with delicious coconut milk.

Yields: 2 Servings

Ingredients:

- 270ml unsweetened almond milk
- 1 frozen banana
- 1 tablespoon virgin coconut oil
- 1 tablespoon shredded coconut

Directions:

1. Pour the almond milk and the ice into the blender and blitz for 15 seconds.
2. Add the rest of the ingredients and blitz until smooth and creamy!
3. Delicious!

Health benefits:

- ✓ Cholesterol Free!
- ✓ Very low in sodium
- ✓ High in manganese
- ✓ High vitamin E
- ✓ Good anti-microbial

Nutritional values per serving: Calories: 116; Total Fat: 8.9g; Cholesterol: 0mg; Sodium: 98mg; Potassium: 231mg; Carbohydrates: 9.4g; Protein: 1.0g

The Spa Facial Smoothie

The Spa Facial Smoothie

This smoothie chock-full of the right stuff to make your skin younger looking and more attractive. Specifically this recipe contains an abundance of carotenoids, which studies have shown not only improve skin tone but also protect the skin from oxidative stress which leads to wrinkles.

Yields: 2 Servings

Ingredients:

- 1 handful of kale
- 115g seedless grapes
- 120lml orange juice - fresh
- ½ frozen banana
- 75g apple – cored, skin on
- 1 teaspoon chia seeds

Directions:

1. Place the ice, orange juice, and the kale in the blender and blitz for 15 seconds.
2. Add the rest of the ingredients and blitz on medium for 10 seconds and then on high until it reaches the desired consistency.
3. Sit back, relax and enjoy!

Health benefits:

- ✓ Very high in vitamins C, B6, and A
- ✓ Very high in manganese
- ✓ High in potassium
- ✓ High in dietary fiber
- ✓ Very low in sodium and saturated fat
- ✓ Cholesterol Free!

Nutritional values per serving: Calories: 135; Total Fat: 0,2g; Cholesterol: 0mg; Sodium: 20mg; Potassium: 488mg; Carbohydrates: 27g; Protein: 1.9g

Natural Botox Smoothie

This smoothie is packed with phytonutrients, minerals and vitamins that will protect and maintain your skins cell membranes. They also reduce inflammation and help protect against sun damage. Drink it regularly for a natural facelift!

Yields: 2 Servings

Ingredients:

- 170g soft tofu
- 55g frozen blueberries
- 45g strawberries
- 60ml cold water
- ¼ teaspoon vanilla extract
- Stevia to taste
- 100g ice

Directions:

1. Place all the ingredients in the blender and blitz until smooth.
2. Sip it slowly. Enjoy!

Health benefits:

- ✓ Cholesterol free!
- ✓ Very low in sodium
- ✓ High in calcium
- ✓ Very high in manganese
- ✓ High in selenium
- ✓ Very high in vitamin B6 and C

Nutritional values per serving: Calories: 130; Total Fat: 5.4g; Cholesterol: 0mg; Sodium: 11mg; Potassium: 205mg; Carbohydrates: 8.9g; Protein: 8.5g

Guacamole Delight Smoothie

Avocadoes have a lot more uses than just making guacamole. They are packed with vitamins K, E and C all of which play an important role in keeping your skin healthy, youthful and beautiful. This smoothie replenishes the skins moisture from within and helps reduce inflammation and puffiness.

Yields: 2 Servings

Ingredients:

- ½ avocado – pitted and peeled
- 1 peach, pitted
- 85g strawberries
- 200ml fat free Greek yoghurt
- 60ml water
- 1 teaspoon grape seed oil (or substitute virgin coconut oil or flaxseed oil)
- 1 teaspoon honey (optional)

Directions:

1. Add all the ingredients to your blender and blitz until smooth.
2. Serve chilled.
3. Scrumptious!

Health benefits:

- ✓ Cholesterol Free!
- ✓ Low in sodium
- ✓ High in vitamin C, K and E

Nutritional values per serving: Calories: 245; Total Fat 16.8g; Cholesterol: 0mg; Sodium: 4mg; Potassium: 394mg; Carbohydrates: 14.6g; Protein: 8.6g

Kale 'Killer Glow' Smoothie

The sheer volume and variety of nutrients in kale has earned it the nickname 'queen of greens'. By adding kale to your smoothies you will be giving your skins health and appearance a huge boost.

Yields: 2 Servings

Ingredients:

- 1 handful of kale
- 120ml lemon juice
- 1 apple – cored, skin on
- 45g parsley
- 360ml coconut water
- 1 celery stick
- Honey or Stevia to taste (optional)

Directions:

1. Add the coconut water, the lemon juice and the kale to the blender and blitz until it is all chopped up.
2. Now add the parsley and then the apple and finally the celery.
3. Blend until smooth adding more coconut water if necessary to achieve your desired consistency. Add some honey or Stevia if desired.
4. Drink this daily and you will be walking around with a radiant glow!

Health benefits:

- ✓ Very high in vitamins A, B6 and C
- ✓ High in potassium and magnesium
- ✓ Very high in manganese
- ✓ High in iron and calcium
- ✓ High in dietary fiber
- ✓ Cholesterol Free!

Nutritional values per serving: Calories: 76; Total Fat: 0.7g; Cholesterol: 0mg; Sodium: 59mg; Potassium: 516mg; Carbohydrates: 15.6g; Protein: 2.6g

Berries for Beauty Smoothie

Berries are packed full of antioxidants which help neutralize the free radicals which damage our bodies and lead to aging. Berries are also loaded with vitamin C which helps with our complexion. These superfoods also help the body produce collagen which makes our skin youthful and soft and minimizes the appearance of fine lines.

Yields: 1 Servings

Ingredients:

- 135ml fat free Greek yoghurt
- 30g blueberries
- 45g strawberries
- 45g raspberries
- A few kale leaves
- 60ml water

Directions:

1. Place all the ingredients in your blender and blitz until smooth and yummy!
2. Consume slowly and revel in the deliciousness!

Health benefits:

- ✓ Very high in vitamin C, B6 and A
- ✓ Very high in manganese
- ✓ High in dietary fiber
- ✓ Very low in sodium
- ✓ Cholesterol Free!
- ✓ Very low in saturated fat

Nutritional values per serving: Calories: 84; Total Fat: 0,5g; Cholesterol: 0g; Sodium: 8mg; Potassium: 212mg; Carbohydrates: 15,8g; Protein: 5.2g

Fantastic Four Smoothie

Spinach, cucumber, celery and apple - these fantastic four ingredients each have their own unique 'super powers' to fight aging, in their own way. Spinach combats free radicals thus keeping your skin supple and wrinkle free. Cucumbers contain anti-inflammatory qualities that will aid the healing of your skin. Being a water food, cucumber will also help keep your skin hydrated. Celery has nutrients which help to lower blood pressure and reduce stress, thereby delaying the aging process. Apples contain many vitamins and beneficial compounds that work to combat oxidative stress, slowing the aging process and promoting healing.

Yield: 2 Servings

Ingredients:

- 1 apple – cored
- ½ cucumber
- 115g spinach
- 115g celery stalks
- 120ml apple juice

Directions:

1. Place all the ingredients in your blender and blitz until smooth.
2. Sip through a straw and enjoy!

Health benefits:

- ✓ Very high in vitamins C, B6 and A
- ✓ High in potassium and iron
- ✓ High in dietary fiber
- ✓ Low in sodium
- ✓ Cholesterol Free!
- ✓ Very low in saturated fat

Nutritional values per serving: Calories: 94; Total Fat: 0.2g; Cholesterol: 0mg; Sodium: 33mg; Potassium: 309mg; Carbohydrates: 17.4g; Protein: 0.7g

Energy Boost Smoothies

Modern life is stressful! We live in an age where there is seldom enough hours in the day to achieve all that we need to do. We seem to run from one thing to another with barely enough time to take a breath in between. It's no wonder then that most of us feel flat, run-down and lacking in energy most of the time. For some, that slump comes mid-morning and for others in the afternoon and it hits you suddenly with no prior warning. There are very few of us that could boast not needing a little more energy to get through the day. This is where smoothies are truly beneficial. Not just quick and easy, but if you pack them full of just the right combination of ingredients, you will have plenty of energy to meet your daily demands.

Scientists, nutritionists and dieticians all agree on one thing and that is that breakfast is the most important meal of the day. It sets the tone for the rest of your day. Scrimp on breakfast and you will be left wanting all day, never quite making up for those all-important lost calories. Start your day off right and you are set until dusk. What better way to start your day than chugging down a delicious, nutritious and energy packed smoothie that will provide you with the necessary get-up-and-go that you need to start your day on the right foot? And if you need to recharge in the afternoon, well that's no problem either. Simply mix up a smoothie packed full of energy boosting ingredients and feel your tired body and muscles revitalize. Energy boosting smoothies are also a great pre-workout drink that provides your body with the extra vooma to really make your workout count without depleting your body.

So never get caught snoozing on your desk again! Here is the 411 on what you need in your smoothies to keep you bright eyed and bushy tailed from dawn until dusk! For an extra boost of energy try supplementing your smoothies with one or more of the following: maca powder, raw cacao powder, chia seeds, coconut (oil, butter, water and flesh), spirulina, goji berries, hemp seeds and oil, flax seeds and oil, oats, broccoli, sesame seeds, spinach, apricots, walnuts, almonds, pomegranate arils and green tea.

Here's to that extra spring in your step – Cheers!

Mint Surprise Smoothie

This smoothie will give you smile in the morning or a welcome energy boost during the day. It is packed with energy from the fruits and the mint gives it a refreshing after taste!

Yields: 2 Servings

Ingredients:

- 1 apple – cored
- 100g pineapple
- 300g frozen watermelon – seeded
- 1 teaspoon lime juice
- Sprig of fresh mint
- Water as needed

Directions:

1. Put the pineapple into the blender first and blitz until smooth.
2. Add the rest of the ingredients and blend until well combined, adding water as needed.
3. Yummy!

Health benefits:

- ✓ Very high in vitamins C, B6 and A
- ✓ Very high in manganese
- ✓ Very low in sodium
- ✓ Cholesterol Free!
- ✓ Very low in saturated fat

Nutritional values per serving: Calories: 117; Total Fat 0.3g; Cholesterol: 0mg; Sodium: 2mg; Potassium: 247mg; Carbohydrates: 20.8g; Protein: 1.2g

Sunshine Glow Smoothie

Sunshine Glow Smoothie

This tangy and sweet smoothie will give you the kick start you need in the morning, and leave you feeling satiated. The dietary fiber will keep you feeling full for longer while the high energy and vitamin content gives you go!

Yields: 2 Servings

Ingredients:

- ½ frozen banana
- 120ml orange juice – freshly juiced
- 115g ruby grapefruit
- 85g strawberries, chopped
- 100g ice

Directions:

1. Add all of the ingredients and blend until smooth.
2. Serve chilled.
3. Amazing!

Health benefits:

- ✓ Very high in vitamins C and A
- ✓ High in vitamin B6
- ✓ High in potassium and magnesium
- ✓ High in dietary fiber
- ✓ Very low in sodium
- ✓ Very low in saturated fat
- ✓ Cholesterol Free!

Nutritional values per serving: Calories: 86; Total Fat: 0.2g; Cholesterol: 0mg; Sodium: 4mg; Potassium: 352mg; Carbohydrates: 21.9g; Protein: 1.4g

Mango Mayhem Smoothie

This smoothie is a must for those who enjoy mangoes! Not only does it taste amazing but it is packed full of energy to get you going in the morning and help sustain your energy throughout the day.

Yields: 2 Servings

Ingredients:

- 400g mango – peeled
- 210ml unsweetened almond milk
- 55g blueberries
- 140g banana
- 1 teaspoon maple syrup (optional)
- Water as needed

Directions:

1. Blitz all the ingredients together in your blender, adding water as needed to reach your desired consistency.
2. Serve over ice.
3. Superb!

Health benefits:

- ✓ High in vitamins C and B6
- ✓ High in manganese
- ✓ Very low sodium
- ✓ Cholesterol Free!

Nutritional values per serving: Calories: 203; Total Fat: 1.4g; Cholesterol: 0mg; Sodium: 70mg; Potassium: 501mg; Carbohydrates: 48.6g; Protein: 1.9g

Supercharge Smoothie

This smoothie has a wonderfully complex flavor, the only drawback being you might want more! It is not too rich so maybe take the second serving with you to have later in the day. It has everything you need to get you going in the morning. It is high in energy and vitamins to leave you feeling supercharged to meet the days challenges.

Yields: 2 Servings

Ingredients:

- 75g blackberries
- 55g blueberries
- ½ frozen banana
- 135ml coconut milk
- 1 teaspoon flaxseed oil
- 1 teaspoon honey

Directions:

1. Add all the ingredients to your blender and blitz until creamy and smooth.
2. Drink it up.
3. Enjoy!

Health benefits:

- ✓ Very high in vitamin B6
- ✓ High in vitamin C
- ✓ High in manganese
- ✓ Very low in sodium
- ✓ Cholesterol Free!

Nutritional values per serving: Calories: 240; Total Fat: 16.9g; Cholesterol: 0mg; Sodium: 10mg; Potassium: 380mg; Carbohydrates: 23.4g; Protein: 2.3g

Green Smoothie Bomb

This powder keg of vitamins is also very low in calories. So if you are looking to lose weight but you still need a hit of sustained energy in the morning this smoothie is the way to go!

Yield: 2 Servings

Ingredients:

- ½ frozen banana
- 115g celery
- 1 handful of kale
- ½ pear – cored
- 1 teaspoon lemon juice
- 120ml water

Directions:

1. Tip all the ingredients into your blender and blitz until smooth.
2. Add more water if the end product is too thick.
3. Chug it down.
4. Start your day!

Health benefits:

- ✓ Very high in vitamins C, B6 and A
- ✓ High in potassium and magnesium
- ✓ High in dietary fiber
- ✓ Very low in saturated fats
- ✓ Cholesterol Free!

Nutritional values per serving: Calories: 59; Total Fat: 0.1g; Cholesterol: 0mg; Sodium: 33mg; Potassium: 300mg; Carbohydrates14.6g; Protein: 1.2g

Aunty Flo's Smoothie

This smoothie is ideal for women who have just given birth or who are feeling the depletory effects of menstruation. This tonic is iron rich and will help your body resupply blood, and help mildly detox the liver. It will also give a healthy energy boost and help rejuvenate tired muscles.

Yields: 2 Servings

Ingredients:

- 2 beets – peeled and chopped
- 45g carrots – chopped
- 1 apple – cored
- A few kale leaves
- 120ml cranberry juice

Directions:

1. Pour the cranberry juice into your blender first and then add the beets and blitz until completely chopped.
2. Add the kale and blitz again until fully chopped.
3. Now add the rest of the ingredients and blend until smooth.
4. Add more water if the smoothie is too thick for your taste.
5. Drink and enjoy!

Health benefits:

- ✓ Very high in vitamins A, B6 and C
- ✓ High in potassium and magnesium
- ✓ Very high in manganese
- ✓ High in dietary fiber
- ✓ Very low in saturated fats
- ✓ Cholesterol Free!

Nutritional values per serving: Calories: 112; Total Fat: 0.1g; Cholesterol: 0mg; Sodium: 81mg; Potassium: 508mg; Carbohydrates: 27.7g; Protein: 1.8g

Wimbledon Smoothie

This strawberries and cream smoothie tastes delicious and is healthy for you too! Make sure you have a playing partner to share it with to take the temptation of the second serving away!

Yields: 2 Servings

Ingredients:

- 140g strawberries
- 180ml coconut milk
- ½ frozen banana
- 1 teaspoon honey (optional)
- 120ml water

Directions:

1. Serve all the ingredients into the blender and smash them until creamy smooth.
2. Tuck in!

Health benefits:

- ✓ Very high in vitamin C
- ✓ High in manganese
- ✓ High in potassium
- ✓ Very low in sodium
- ✓ Cholesterol Free!

Nutritional values per serving: Calories: 274; Total Fat: 21.7g; Cholesterol: 0mg; Sodium: 15mg; Potassium: 483mg; Carbohydrates: 21.9g; Protein: 2.9g

Everything's Peachy Smoothie

This is a seriously peachy smoothie! You can make this smoothie the night before you need it and leave it in the refrigerator. There is no way you are going to oversleep with this baby waiting for you in the morning! It will also give you an energy boost to keep your brain functioning.

Yields: 2 Servings

Ingredients:

- 1 peach – pitted and peeled
- 55g raspberries
- 135ml fat free Greek yoghurt
- 135ml unsweetened almond milk

Directions:

1. Pour all the ingredients into the blender and blitz until smooth.
2. Chill and serve within 1 to 2 days of making.
3. Simply Divine!

Health benefits:

- ✓ High in vitamin C
- ✓ High in manganese
- ✓ Very low in sodium
- ✓ Cholesterol Free!

Nutritional values per serving: Calories: 204; Total Fat: 14.7g; Cholesterol: 0mg; Sodium: 9mg; Potassium: 325mg; Carbohydrates: 15.9g; Protein: 5.6g

The Booster Smoothie

For a big boost in the morning or after a work-out it doesn't get much better than this! This smoothie ticks all the boxes, it is high in energy, low in calories, high in vitamins, and low in saturated fats. It is really one of the best energy booster smoothies you can make!

Yields: 2 Servings

Ingredients:

- 75g blackberries
- 75g currants/raisins
- 1 frozen banana
- 1 orange – peeled
- 2 handfuls of baby spinach
- ½ cup apple juice

Directions:

1. Fire all the ingredients into your blender and blast them together until smooth.
2. Serve chilled.
3. Energize!

Health benefits:

- ✓ Very high in vitamin A and C
- ✓ High in potassium and manganese
- ✓ Very high in dietary fiber

- ✓ Very low in saturated fats
- ✓ Low in sodium
- ✓ Cholesterol Free!

Nutritional values per serving: Calories: 235; Total Fats: 0.6g; Cholesterol: 0mg; Sodium: 30mg; Potassium: 869mg; Carbohydrates: 59.6g; Protein: 3.5g

Fruit Salad Smoothie

This smoothie is a great all-rounder. It has great amounts of energy for you as well as being high in fiber and vitamins. Its low calorie count will also help you maintain your weight goals.

Yields: 2 Servings

Ingredients:

- 85g pineapple
- 1 orange – peeled
- ½ frozen banana
- 1 small apple – cored
- 75g blackberries

Directions:

1. Toss all the ingredients into your blender and blitz until smooth.
2. Serve immediately.
3. Enjoy!

Health benefits:

- ✓ Very high in vitamins C and B6
- ✓ Very high in manganese
- ✓ Very high in dietary fiber

- ✓ Very low in sodium
- ✓ Very low in saturated fats
- ✓ Cholesterol Free!

Nutritional values per serving: Calories: 144; Total Fat: 0.3g; Cholesterol: 0mg; Sodium: 4mg; Potassium: 456mg; Carbohydrates: 36.7; Protein: 1.9g

Super Weight Loss Smoothies

Although each and every wonderful smoothie in this book is low in calories, I thought I'd create this section specifically for those who want to focus on weight loss. Most of us have nothing short of a love/hate relationship with dieting and calories. We all know that restricting our calories to a point is necessary, but few of us enjoy the deprivation that comes hand in hand with being able to fit into your skinny jeans comfortably.

Snacking between meals is more often than not the death knell of even the most well-meaning of dieter's intentions to stay on the straight and narrow. Most of us are more than capable of sticking to healthy food at mealtimes, but few of us can resist the rumblings and grumblings of hunger pangs that strike mid-morning and mid-afternoon and this is where most diets are derailed in the blink of an eye. Sitting in your office, feeling faint from hunger (healthy salad lunches don't go far!) and suddenly the sandwich lady comes around or you visit the bathroom which happens to be situated next to the office vending machine and before you know it, you are inhaling a sandwich or a candy bar, then spending the rest of the afternoon cocooned in guilt and self-loathing for once again succumbing to your weak resolve. What to do?

What if I told you that you could enjoy something delicious, filling and low calorie? Don't shake your head, it is possible! The smoothie recipes that follow are crammed full of delicious goodness, without the calories. With each one weighing in at under 200 calories (and many under 100 calories), you will be hard pressed to find a better in-between meal snack that will tide you over to your next meal. And when you throw in some of the following ingredients that are specifically designed to accelerate and promote weight loss, well, you have nothing short of a winning combination.

Apples, spinach, goji berries, blueberries, pomegranates, tarragon, kale, almonds, sesame seeds, hemp seeds, pine nuts, chilies, dandelion root, green tea, grapefruit, cayenne pepper, plantains, celery, raw cacao, cinnamon and maca powder, all kick your metabolism up a notch and speed up your weight loss efforts. So feel free to add these ingredients to the recipes listed below if you have them at hand.

Drink up and feel the pounds melt away!

Really Rhubarb Smoothie

You can serve this smoothie for dessert because it looks and tastes so great! It is low in calories and fat so is ideal for those on a weight loss or maintenance program. Enjoy this smoothie day or night, whenever the hunger pangs strike!

Yields: 1 Serving

Ingredients:

- 60g rhubarb stalks – chopped
- 140g mango - chopped
- 1 tablespoon honey
- 170g fat free Greek yoghurt
- 120ml water
- 100g ice

Directions:

1. Cover the rhubarb and microwave until soft, chop it and place it into a measuring cup.
2. Add all the ingredients to your blender and blitz until smooth.
3. Add a splash of water if it is too thick for your liking.
4. Delicious!

Health benefits:

- ✓ Cholesterol free!
- ✓ Very high in Vitamin C
- ✓ Very low in sodium
- ✓ Very low in saturated fat

Nutritional values per serving: Calories: 138; Total fat: 0.3g; Cholesterol: 0mg; Sodium: 5mg; Potassium: 85mg; Carbohydrates: 17g; Protein: 7.8g

Banana Spice and Everything Nice

This smoothie is nice and bulky, yet low in calories, so it will fill you up nicely and keep you satiated until your next meal. It is the perfect in between meal snack for those on a calorie restricted diet plan. It might be a bit spicy the first time you try it, which is why I recommend adding the spices to taste.

Yields: 1 Serving

Ingredients:

- 1 frozen banana
- ½ teaspoon ground nutmeg – or to taste
- ½ teaspoon ground cloves – or to taste
- ½ teaspoon ground cinnamon – or to taste
- 180ml unsweetened almond milk

Directions:

1. Place the banana, the almond milk and the ice into your blender and blitz until smooth.
2. Start adding in the nutmeg, the cloves and the cinnamon in pinches and blitzing further, until you are satisfied with the quantities.
3. Drink and enjoy!

Health benefits:

- ✓ Very high in vitamins E and B12
- ✓ High in vitamin C and B6
- ✓ Very high in manganese and calcium
- ✓ High in riboflavin
- ✓ High in dietary fiber
- ✓ Low in saturated fats
- ✓ Cholesterol Free!

Nutritional values per serving: Calories: 135; Total Fats: 2.5g; Cholesterol: 0mg; Sodium: 118mg; Potassium: 469mg; Carbohydrates: 28.5g; Protein: 2.0g

Bluebell Smoothie

This flavorful smoothie is so yummy it should be called dessert! It is also guilt free because of the low calorie count. It has just the right amount of fats to keep your brain functioning at peak levels and ward off fatigue until it is time for your next meal.

Yields: 1 Serving

Ingredients:

- 115g celery stalks – chopped
- 55g frozen blueberries
- 180ml unsweetened almond milk
- 170g fat free Greek yoghurt
- 1 teaspoon vanilla extract
- Stevia to taste

Directions:

1. Place all the ingredients into your blender and blitz until smooth.
2. Drink and enjoy!

Health benefits:

- ✓ Very high in Vitamin B6, C, and E
- ✓ Very high in calcium
- ✓ Very low in saturated fat
- ✓ Cholesterol Free!

Nutritional values per serving: Calories: 189; Total Fats: 2.2g; Cholesterol: 0mg; Sodium: 178mg; Potassium: 315mg; Carbohydrates: 12.8g; Protein: 8.6g

The Strawbeet Smoothie

The Strawbeet Smoothie

This delicious low calorie smoothie has a good quantity of fiber to aid digestion. Thanks to the beets it also has a nice helping of carbs for energy. The coconut water helps to replenish and revitalize and adds a yummy flavor dimension too.

Yields: 1 Serving

Ingredients:

- 1 beet – peeled, steamed and chopped
- 180ml coconut water – unsweetened
- 100g frozen strawberries
- 60ml lime juice

Directions:

1. Peel the beets and steam them until they are tender.
2. Add all the ingredients to your blender and blitz them until they are smooth.
3. Drink it up.
4. Enjoy!

Health benefits:

- ✓ Very high in vitamin C
- ✓ Very high in potassium
- ✓ Very high in manganese
- ✓ Very high in dietary fiber
- ✓ High in magnesium
- ✓ Low in saturated fat
- ✓ Cholesterol Free!

Nutritional values per serving: Calories: 106; Total Fats: 0.8g; Cholesterol: 0mg; Sodium: 256mg; Potassium: 874mg; Carbohydrates: 23.5g; Protein: 3.5g

Blackberry Bomber

This smoothie is the bomb dude! It is high in dietary fiber and vitamins, low in calories and tastes awesome too! So enjoy the bomb of antioxidants bombarding your system as you sip on this delicious smoothie.

Yields: 1 Serving

Ingredients:

- 140g blackberries
- 135ml fat free Greek yoghurt
- 60ml orange juice – fresh
- 1 tablespoon honey

Directions:

1. Rinse the blackberries and place them in the blender with the other ingredients and blitz until smooth.
2. Pour, add a straw and sip!

Health benefits:

- ✓ Very high in vitamins C and B6
- ✓ Very high in manganese
- ✓ Very high in dietary fiber
- ✓ Very low in sodium
- ✓ Very low in saturated fats
- ✓ Cholesterol Free!

Nutritional values per serving: Calories: 154; Total Fats: 0.8g; Cholesterol: 0mg; Sodium: 3mg; Potassium: 368mg; Carbohydrates: 37.6g; Protein: 7.5g

Appleberry Smoothie

This delicious ultra-low calorie smoothie is a must for those of us trying to lose weight and remain healthy. It is packed with vitamins and fiber whilst being super low in fats. A guilt free snack to enjoy between meals!

Yields: 2 Servings

Ingredients:

- 1 apple – cored
- 60g blueberries
- 35g strawberries – hulled
- 240ml cranberry juice
- 1 tablespoon maple syrup
- 115g crushed ice

Directions:

1. Toss the ingredients into your blender and blitz until yummy!
2. Sip and Enjoy!

Health benefits:

- ✓ Very high in vitamins C and B6
- ✓ Very high in manganese
- ✓ High in dietary fiber
- ✓ Low in sodium
- ✓ No saturated fats
- ✓ Cholesterol Free!

Nutritional values per serving: Calories: 160; Total Fats: 0.1g; Cholesterol: 0mg; Sodium: 2mg; Potassium: 173mg; Carbohydrates: 25.9g; Protein: 0.3g

Greek Lassi Smoothie

No it is not a Scots-Greek inspired smoothie! A Lassi is a traditional Indian drink served sweet or salty. Yoghurt, mango and vegetables are the usual main ingredients, depending on whether sweet or salty. It is low in calories with a nice amount of protein and fiber to still nourish you while the pounds melt away.

Yields: 2 Servings

Ingredients:

- ½ large mango – peeled, pitted and chopped
- 135ml Greek yoghurt – fat free, plain
- 210ml water
- ¼ teaspoon ginger – freshly sliced
- Stevia to taste

Directions:

1. Add all the ingredients to the blender and blitz until smooth.
2. Sip slowly and enjoy!

Health benefits:

- ✓ High in vitamin C
- ✓ Very low in sodium
- ✓ Very low in saturated fats
- ✓ Cholesterol Free!

Nutritional values per serving: Calories: 120; Total Fats: 0.2g; Cholesterol: 0mg; Sodium: 5mg; Potassium: 166mg; Carbohydrates: 17.8g; Protein: 8g

Gingerberry Smoothie

This is a very low-calorie, super-healthy and tasty smoothie. It is ideal for a weight loss program or as a between meal snack. The combination of ginger, honey and coconut water adds a complex interplay of flavors that will quickly make this smoothie one of your all time weight-loss favorites.

Yields: 2 Servings

Ingredients:

- 1 pear, cored and quartered
- 55g frozen cranberries
- 240ml coconut water
- ¼ teaspoon ground ginger
- ½ tablespoon honey

Directions:

1. Transfer all the ingredients to the blender and blitz them until smooth.
2. Pour into a glass and enjoy!

Health benefits:

- ✓ Very high in vitamin C
- ✓ High in potassium
- ✓ High in dietary fiber
- ✓ Low in saturated fat
- ✓ Cholesterol Free!

Nutritional values per serving: Calories: 91; Total Fat: 0.4g; Cholesterol: 0mg; Sodium: 127mg; Potassium: 409mg; Carbohydrates: 22.6g; Protein: 1.2g

Popeye Surprise

Popeye Surprise

This smoothie would give Popeye a welcome surprise. Between the strawberries and the banana you would be surprised to find out that there is such a hefty helping of spinach in this nutritionally packed and deliciously drinkable treat. Add ice blocks instead of water to turn this into a delectable after dinner dessert. YUM!

Yields: 2 Servings

Ingredients:

- 1 handful of spinach – chopped
- 45g strawberries – sliced
- 1 frozen banana
- 60g fat free Greek yoghurt
- 120ml water

Directions:

1. Place all the ingredients into your blender and blitz until smooth, adding more water to thin the consistency if desired.
2. Pour, drink and enjoy!

Health benefits:

- ✓ Very high in vitamins C and A
- ✓ High in manganese
- ✓ Very low in sodium
- ✓ Very low in saturated fat
- ✓ Cholesterol Free!

Nutritional values per serving: Calories: 79; Total Fats: 0.2g; Cholesterol: 0mg; Sodium: 11mg; Potassium: 225mg; Carbohydrates: 12.7g; Protein: 3.5g

Avonana Smoothie

This smoothie has a wonderful kaleidoscope of flavors. It is very good for you too! It is rich in vitamins and fiber which are essential when following a calorie restricted diet. Fiber helps to ward off the hunger pangs that will send you to the nearest vending machine so include this smoothie in your diet repertoire often to fight those snack attacks!

Yields: 2 Servings

Ingredients:

- ½ avocado – pitted and peeled
- ½ frozen banana
- 30g blueberries
- 60g raspberries
- 1 handful baby spinach
- 1 teaspoon raw honey
- 180ml unsweetened almond milk
- Pinch of cayenne

Directions:

1. Place all the ingredients in your blender and blitz until delicious.
2. This one will become a firm favorite with the yummy chocolate notes!

Health benefits:

- ✓ Very high in B6
- ✓ High in vitamin C
- ✓ High in dietary fiber
- ✓ Very low in sodium
- ✓ Cholesterol Free!

Nutritional values per serving: Calories: 162; Total Fat: 10.5g; Cholesterol: 0mg; Sodium: 74mg; Potassium: 452mg; Carbohydrates: 18.8g; Protein 1.8g

Citrus Delights

This refreshing smoothie is vitamin rich and high in fiber. It is also low in fats and calories, making it an essential part of any calorie controlled eating plan. This is a wonderful pick-me-up for Monday mornings after a busy weekend or as an after workout snack as it replenishes and revitalizes the body beautifully.

Yields: 1 Serving

Ingredients:

- 1 orange – peeled
- 1 peach – pip removed
- 180ml coconut water
- 1 tsp lemon juice
- 55g carrots – peeled and chopped
- 1 handful of spinach
- 100g ice

Directions:

1. Toss it all in your blender and blitz away until smooth.

Health benefits:

- ✓ Very high in vitamins C and A
- ✓ High in potassium
- ✓ High in dietary fiber
- ✓ High in magnesium
- ✓ Very low in saturated fats
- ✓ Cholesterol Free!

Nutritional values per serving: Calories: 173; Total Fats: 0.9g; Cholesterol: 0mg; Sodium: 215mg; Potassium: 1105mg; Carbohydrates: 40.7g; Protein: 4.4g

Peach Pudding Smoothie

This super low-calorie smoothie has everything you look for in a smoothie. Great taste, easy to assemble, and vitamin stuffed to keep you healthy. And it masquerades as a delicious healthy dessert!

Yields: 2 Servings

Ingredients:

- ½ large peach, chopped
- 120ml unsweetened almond milk
- 210ml fat free Greek yoghurt
- 1 single graham cracker rectangle
- 1 tsp cinnamon
- ½ tsp vanilla extract
- pinch of nutmeg
- Stevia to taste
- 100g ice

Directions:

1. Place all the ingredients into your blender and blitz thoroughly until smooth.
2. For an even better taste, garnish with another crumbled graham cracker on top.
3. Drink immediately and enjoy!

Health benefits:

- ✓ High in vitamin E and phosphorus
- ✓ High in calcium & magnesium
- ✓ Low in saturated fat
- ✓ Very low in cholesterol

Nutritional values per serving: Calories: 189; Total Fats: 4.3g; Cholesterol: 2mg; Sodium: 252mg; Potassium: 553mg; Carbohydrates: 23.6g; Protein: 12.5g

Dr. Jarvis Smoothie

An apple a day keeps the doctor away. Apples are packed with vitamins, fiber and a host of other beneficial properties. Blueberries are a superfood that make any smoothie a cracker. This smoothie is also very low-calorie and thus great for calorie restricted diets. The apple cider vinegar adds a subtle yet interesting taste dimension and tips the scales favorably on the side of nutrition.

Yields: 2 Servings

Ingredients:

- 1 apple – peeled and cored
- 55g frozen blueberries
- 100g grapes – seedless
- 120ml water
- ½ teaspoon apple cider vinegar – with the mother in

Directions:

1. Throw all the ice and fruit into your blender and blitz until smooth.
2. Drink and feel slimmer!

Health benefits:

- ✓ Very high in vitamins B6 and C
- ✓ High in manganese
- ✓ High in dietary fiber

- ✓ Very low in sodium
- ✓ Very low in saturated fats
- ✓ Cholesterol Free!

Nutritional values per serving: Calories: 69; Total Fats: 0.2g; Cholesterol: 0mg; Sodium: 2mg; Potassium: 102mg; Carbohydrates 13.7g; Protein: 0.4g

Cleanse and Detox Smoothies

Detoxing is the current buzzword on everybody's lips! And it is hardly surprising when you consider the world we live in – let's be honest, it's dirty! Our water is full of chemicals to make it "pure", the air we breathe is chock full of pollutants, our food is either sprayed with pesticides or pumped full of hormones and honorable mention should be given to our fast food industry which packs our food full of additives and preservatives and processes it so heavily all under the guise of "convenience". The rapid rise in the detox craze is due to the fact that many believe that as a result of our rapid development, our bodies, which are naturally geared towards detoxification, are simply not coping with the onslaught of all the chemical substances that now exist in our world. Consequently, consuming certain things helps to support the body's natural process of detoxing and helps to make it more efficient.

Detoxing literally means "to cleanse" and rests on the premise that the body needs to be purged of toxins on a regular basis so that it can function optimally. Detoxing basically works to boost the efficiency of the digestive system – by clearing out the toxins, the digestive system is better able to absorb the necessary nutrients from food that will nourish the body properly. With the increase in everything artificial, more and more people are embarking on juice cleanses, fasts and detox diets. These can be a little extreme and while they do serve their purpose of ridding the body of toxins, they often come hand in hand with some nasty side effects that can make your 3 day fast feel like 3 weeks!

However, if you live a healthy lifestyle and simply include one of these smoothies in your diet on a regular basis, there will be no need to embark on any of these drastic diets and cleanses. Detoxing is all about purging your body of the bad and replacing it with goodness that nourishes your body from the inside out. What better way to do this than with ingredients such as acai berries, goji berries, coconut water, pomegranates, lemons, cucumbers, cranberries, blueberries, apples, beets, turmeric, garlic, ginger, cayenne pepper, cilantro, parsley, mint, cinnamon and green tea. Include one or more of these ingredients to the following basic smoothie recipes and really feel the difference – clean on the inside, healthy on the outside!

Strawberries Forever Smoothie

Strawberries are packed full of phytonutrients and supply our bodies with significant doses of antioxidants and anti-inflammatories. Besides helping our bodies deal with toxins they also taste great! The spinach, banana and orange help round out this vitamin packed smoothie.

Yields: 2 Servings

Ingredients:

- 155g strawberries, halved
- 1 frozen banana
- 1 orange – peeled and segmented
- 120ml water
- 1 tablespoon lemon zest
- 1 handful of spinach

Directions:

1. Throw it all in the blender and blitz until smooth.
2. Drink it while it's yummy!

Health benefits:

- ✓ Very high in vitamin C
- ✓ High in vitamin A
- ✓ High in magnesium and manganese
- ✓ High in dietary fiber
- ✓ Low in saturated fat
- ✓ Cholesterol Free!

Nutritional values per serving: Calories: 123; Total Fats: 0.4g; Cholesterol: 0mg; Sodium: 9mg; Potassium: 539mg; Carbohydrates: 30.7g; Protein: 2.2g

Avo Goddess Smoothie

The avocado, kale, cucumber, and coconut water will cleanse and shower your cells with alkalinizing goodness. A slightly alkaline inner body environment allows your body's immune system to operate optimally. This allows it to flush away toxins effectively. The blueberries are also packed with antioxidants and fiber which will aid the process. The potassium and other vitamins in the banana round out the positive impact of this smoothie on your body.

Yields: 2 Servings

Ingredients:

- ½ avocado – pitted and peeled
- ½ frozen banana
- 100g blueberries
- ½ cucumber
- 1 small handful of kale
- 120ml coconut water

Directions:

1. Throw it all in the blender and blitz until smooth.
2. Drink it all.
3. Feel cleansed!

Health benefits:

- ✓ Very high in vitamins C and B6
- ✓ High in vitamin A
- ✓ High in manganese
- ✓ High in dietary fiber
- ✓ Very low sodium
- ✓ Cholesterol Free!

Nutritional values per serving: Calories: 194; Total Fats: 10.1g; Cholesterol: 0mg; Sodium: 9mg; Potassium: 557mg; Carbohydrates: 25.1g; Protein: 2.5g

Glorious Green Smoothie

This is a brilliant low calorie detox and cleanse smoothie. It is high in dietary fiber which binds to free radicals in our digestive tract and neutralizes them until they are eliminated. The cucumber also contains a diuretic to help your kidneys flush out impurities. It also contains a variety of vitamins and minerals to fortify the body.

Yields: 2 Servings

Ingredients:

- ½ cucumber
- 1 small handful of kale
- 6 large strawberries
- 1 pear, chopped
- 115g celery stalks
- 100g frozen broccoli
- 60ml lemon juice
- 240ml water

Directions:

1. Throw it all in the blender and blitz until smooth.
2. Chug it down.
3. Glow from within.

Health benefits:

- ✓ Very high in vitamins A, B6, and C
- ✓ Very high in potassium
- ✓ High in manganese
- ✓ Low in saturated fat
- ✓ High in dietary fiber
- ✓ Cholesterol Free!

Nutritional values per serving: Calories: 92; Total Fats: 0.6g; Cholesterol: 0mg; Sodium: 40mg; Potassium: 498mg; Carbohydrates: 21.5g; Protein: 2.3g

Berrylicious Breakfast Smoothie

Berrylicious Breakfast Smoothie

Don't let the cute name fool you. This is a powerful detoxifying smoothie! The berries turn on strong detoxifying enzymes in our bodies and the ginger promotes digestion. The flaxseed and the soy milk provide a helpful dose of protein to strengthen your body, while the lemon juice and honey raise up the vitamin content.

Yields: 2 Servings

Ingredients:

- 240ml soy milk
- 115g raspberries
- 45g cherries
- 1 tablespoon honey
- 2 teaspoons ginger – grated fine
- 1 tablespoon flaxseed – ground
- 1 tablespoon lemon juice

Directions:

1. Place all the ingredients into the blender and blitz until ready to drink.
2. Enjoy – it's YUMMY!

Health benefits:

- ✓ Very high in B6
- ✓ High in vitamin C
- ✓ High in manganese
- ✓ Low in sodium
- ✓ Low in saturated fats
- ✓ Cholesterol Free!

Nutritional values per serving: Calories: 243; Total Fats: 3.9g; Cholesterol: 0mg; Sodium: 80mg; Potassium: 384mg; Carbohydrates: 47.1g; Protein: 5.9g

Jicama Smoothie

This green smoothie stars the Mexican crunchy root vegetable jicama. The jicama root contains high quantities of vitamins C, A and some of the B's. It also contains significant amounts of phosphorus and calcium. It is high in dietary fiber and is also a prebiotic.

Yields: 2 Servings

Ingredients:

- 65g jicama
- ½ green apple
- ½ avocado – pitted and peeled
- ½ cucumber
- 60ml lime juice
- 240ml water
- 6 Romaine lettuce leaves
- 100g ice
- Stevia to taste

Directions:

1. Throw it all in the blender and blitz until smooth.
2. Drink and enjoy!

Health benefits:

- ✓ Very high in vitamin B6 and C
- ✓ High in dietary fiber
- ✓ Very low in sodium
- ✓ Cholesterol Free!

Nutritional values per serving: Calories: 157; Total Fats: 9.9g; Cholesterol: 0mg; Sodium: 11mg; Potassium: 470mg; Carbohydrates: 16.3g; Protein: 1.7g

Papaya Belly Soother Smoothie

Treat your digestive system to a welcome influx of probiotics from tangy kefir. This is a cultured and fermented drink similar to yoghurt. Papaya is known to aid digestive health, while the lime juice raises the vitamin C content. A healthy strong digestive system can deal effectively with the day to day toxins we ingest.

Yields: 2 Servings

Ingredients:

- 140g papaya
- 240ml coconut kefir (or coconut milk)
- 55g lime juice
- 35g raisins
- 1 tablespoon honey
- 100g ice

Directions:

1. Introduce all the components into the blender and blitz until smooth.
2. Sip it through a straw.
3. Enjoy!

Health benefits:

- ✓ Very high in vitamin C
- ✓ High in vitamins A
- ✓ Very low in sodium
- ✓ Cholesterol Free!

Nutritional values per serving: Calories: 122; Total Fats: 0.3g; Cholesterol: 0mg; Sodium: 12mg; Potassium: 275mg; Carbohydrates: 30.9g; Protein: 10.9g

Alkaline Blast Smoothie

All the movie stars these days are following the alkaline diet. Put simply our bodies normal pH varies between slightly acidic to slightly alkaline depending on what we eat. The western diet that most of us eat tends to leave our bodies in an acidic state most of the time. We need to balance our pH out for it to be healthy.

Yields: 2 Servings

Ingredients:

- 1 pear
- ½ avocado – pitted and peeled
- 1 handful of spinach
- 60ml coconut water
- 240ml soy milk
- 1 teaspoon chia seeds – ground
- 1 tablespoon pumpkin seeds

Directions:

1. Introduce all the components into the blender and blitz until smooth.
2. Drink.
3. Relax.
4. Enjoy!

Health benefits:

- ✓ High in vitamins A and B6
- ✓ High in manganese
- ✓ High in dietary fiber
- ✓ Low in sodium
- ✓ Cholesterol Free!

Nutritional values per serving: Calories: 257; Total Fats: 14.9g; Cholesterol: 0mg; Sodium: 118mg; Potassium: 677mg; Carbohydrates: 25g; Protein: 7.46g

Spiru Smoothie

Spirulina is a form of micro algae. So don't be put off by its dark color and mossy smell, it is a powerful healing and detox agent. The blueberries and the avocado combine with the Spirulina to form a triumvirate of detoxifying agents to cleanse your system leaving you feeling healthy and energized!

Yields: 2 Servings

Ingredients:

- 1 tablespoon Spirulina
- 1 frozen banana
- 55g blueberries
- ½ avocado – pitted and peeled
- 120ml soy milk

Directions:

1. Combine all the ingredients together in the blender and blitz until smooth.
2. Drink and be healthy!

Health benefits:

- ✓ Very high in vitamin B6
- ✓ High in vitamin C
- ✓ High in manganese
- ✓ High in dietary fiber
- ✓ Low in sodium
- ✓ Cholesterol Free!

Nutritional values per serving: Calories: 222; Total Fats: 11.3g; Cholesterol: 0mg; Sodium: 82mg; Potassium: 561mg; Carbohydrates: 28.3g; Protein: 6.4g

King Kale Smoothie

This delicious well rounded smoothie is nicely stocked with both detoxifying ingredients and highly nutritious superfoods. The coconut water and the cucumber are good diuretics, while the high fiber content in the smoothie binds together with toxins in your body and then facilitates elimination.

Yields: 2 Servings

Ingredients:

- 1 handful of kale
- 1 pear
- 1 orange
- ½ banana
- ½ cucumber
- 60ml lemon juice
- 120ml coconut water
- 1 tablespoon hemp seeds
- 1 teaspoon ginger – ground

Directions:

1. Combine this interesting array of ingredients in your blender and blitz until palatable.
2. Drink it up.
3. Delicious!

Health benefits:

- ✓ Very high in vitamins A, B6, and C
- ✓ Very high in manganese
- ✓ Low in saturated fat and sodium
- ✓ High in potassium
- ✓ High in dietary fiber
- ✓ Cholesterol Free!

Nutritional values per serving: Calories: 193; Total Fats: 0.6g; Cholesterol: 0mg; Sodium: 30mg; Potassium: 795mg; Carbohydrates: 39.5g; Protein: 3.7g

Grapefruit Spinach Detox Smoothie

Grapefruit is a great system cleanser and metabolism booster. The high fiber content of this smoothie will also help by binding to all the toxins in your digestive tract. You will then be able to remove them when you eliminate waste.

Yields: 2 Servings

Ingredients:

- 1 grapefruit
- 1 handful of spinach
- 45g red grapes – seedless
- 1 frozen banana
- 1 teaspoon ginger – ground
- 1 Medjool date
- 120ml water

Directions:

1. Toss all the ingredients into your blender and blitz until smooth.
2. Drink and be merry!

Health benefits:

- ✓ Very high in vitamins A and C
- ✓ High in manganese
- ✓ High in dietary fiber
- ✓ Very low in sodium
- ✓ Very low in saturated fat
- ✓ Cholesterol Free!

Nutritional values per serving: Calories: 100; Total Fats: 0.2g; Cholesterol: 0mg; Sodium: 15mg; Potassium 330mg; Carbohydrates: 27.1; Protein: 1.7g

The Fabulous Green Smoothie

This delicious smoothie also moonlights as a powerful detox drink. The parsley and celery that contribute to its green color are also diuretics that help the body wash toxins from our systems. The mango and kale are superfoods stacked with nutrition that will support your body while it is cleansed.

Yields: 2 Servings

Ingredients:

- ½ large mango
- 1 handful of kale – rib and stems removed
- 240ml orange juice
- 15g parsley – chopped
- 15g mint – chopped
- 2 ribs celery - chopped

Directions:

1. Tip all the ingredients into your food processor and blitz until smooth.
2. Sip and enjoy!

Health benefits:

- ✓ Very high in vitamins A, B6, and C
- ✓ High in potassium & iron
- ✓ High in manganese
- ✓ Low in sodium
- ✓ Very low in saturated fats
- ✓ Cholesterol Free!

Nutritional values per serving: Calories: 183; Total Fats: 0.7g; Cholesterol: 0mg; Sodium: 57mg; Potassium: 773mg; Carbohydrates: 36.6g; Protein: 3.3g

Brain Boosting Smoothies

When a person's diet is lacking in certain nutrients, it can actually be toxic to our brains. Just like the rest of your body, your brain needs to be cared for if it is going to perform at its peak.

So what exactly does our brain need to optimize our functioning? The brain is an incredibly active and hungry organ, but is actually quite a "fussy eater". Accordingly, it requires a specific diet abundant in the right substances to aid operation and prevent brain drain!

The best way to provide a constant source of energy for our brains is to eat little and often. Smoothies are a great way to do this as they are quick and easy to prepare and are great between meal snacks or even meal replacements for very busy people who don't have time to cook 3 meals a day.

Protein is broken down into amino acids and these are also essential for the production of neurotransmitters. Neurotransmitters are chemicals that are responsible for relaying messages to the body from the brain and are thus crucial to our ability to do anything. Excellent sources of protein to include in your smoothies are eggs, milk, yoghurt, green leafy vegetables, nuts, and seeds.

Including the right kinds of fat in your diet is important to keep the brain running smoothly. Omega-3 and Omega-6 are found in seaweed, nuts (especially walnuts), seeds (especially flaxseeds and pumpkin seeds), avocados, milk (especially soy milk), coconut oil, and olive oil and are great components to include in your smoothies.

The brain also needs vitamins, minerals and antioxidants. The primary source of these micronutrients is from fruit and vegetables. It is best to include a wide variety of different fruits and vegetables – the more colorful, the better and to choose organic when possible. Cranberries, strawberries, blueberries, blackcurrants, broccoli, grape juice, and pomegranate juice are great brain foods and also powerful antioxidants that protect the brain from damage from free radicals by neutralizing them.

In addition to the right foods, adequate hydration is integral to brain health. So make sure to add water and coconut water especially to your smoothies. Green tea is a great substitute for milk as it contains chemicals that enhance mental alertness without being addictive. There are also a number of herbs and spices that are thought to enhance mental functioning. If you are able to find some of these include them in your smoothies for a super brain boost – gingko biloba, ginseng, gotu kola, sage, turmeric, basil, and rosemary as well as peppermint essential oil.

If you want a brain that operates efficiently at top speed, then it is up to you to provide the correct building blocks through a healthy balanced diet!

Minty Green Smoothie

This decorative and complex flavored green smoothie has all the right stuff for your brain. The right amount of fats from the coconut oil. The right amount of protein from the Greek yoghurt. The right amounts of carbohydrates from the fruits. Put it all together and you have a delicious smoothie that will keep your brain functioning at its peak!

Yields: 1 Serving

Ingredients:

- 2 kiwi fruit – peeled
- ½ apple – chopped
- 130g fat free Greek yoghurt
- ½ cucumber
- 1 handful of spinach (optional)
- 15g mint leaves
- 2 tablespoons virgin coconut oil

Directions:

1. Throw everything into your blender and blitz until yummy.
2. Serve chilled and enjoy!

Health benefits:

- ✓ Very high in vitamins B6 and C
- ✓ High in vitamin A
- ✓ High in iron
- ✓ High in dietary fiber
- ✓ Very low in sodium
- ✓ Cholesterol Free!

Nutritional values per serving: Calories: 427; Total Fats: 28.8g; Cholesterol: 0mg; Sodium: 32mg; Potassium: 960mg; Carbohydrates: 41.2g; Protein: 11.1g

Carrot and Kale Smoothie

A Harvard Medical School study consisting of over 13 000 women, revealed that those who ate higher amounts of cruciferous vegetables like spinach, broccoli and kale had brains that showed less signs of aging than other subjects. So enjoy this smoothie every day for a younger and more vibrant brain.

Yields: 2 Servings

Ingredients:

- 2 whole carrots – chopped
- 1 apple – cored
- 120ml orange juice
- 1 handful of kale – ribs and stem removed
- ½ frozen banana
- 55g broccoli – chopped

Directions:

1. Introduce all the ingredients into your blender one at a time and blitz them together until smooth.
2. Sip and enjoy!

Health benefits:

- ✓ Very high in vitamins A, B6 and C
- ✓ High in potassium
- ✓ High in dietary fiber
- ✓ Very low in saturated fats
- ✓ Low in sodium
- ✓ Cholesterol Free!

Nutritional values per serving: Calories: 147; Total Fats: 0.2g; Cholesterol: 0mg; Sodium: 62mg; Potassium: 722mg; Carbohydrates: 36g; Protein: 2.5g

Almond Spice Smoothie

Almonds have a high protein and dopamine content, giving your mind a boost in focus and motivation. The cinnamon also works on keeping your blood sugar steady thereby allowing your brain to function consistently throughout the day. Plus, this smoothie is to die for!

Yields: 2 Servings

Ingredients:

- 1 frozen banana
- 210ml unsweetened almond milk
- 4 tablespoons organic almond butter (or use organic peanut butter)
- 1 handful of kale – stems removed (optional)
- ¼ teaspoon cinnamon
- ¼ teaspoon nutmeg
- 1 teaspoon vanilla extract
- 1 teaspoon honey

Directions:

1. Add all the ingredients to your blender and blend until smooth.
2. Enjoy immediately – Yum!

Health benefits:

- ✓ Very high in Vitamin A, B6, and C
- ✓ High in manganese
- ✓ Cholesterol Free!

Nutritional values per serving: Calories: 292; Total Fats: 17.6; Cholesterol: 0mg; Sodium: 254mg; Potassium: 636mg; Carbohydrates: 27.3g; Protein: 10.2g

Green Tea Smoothie

Green tea is well known for its antioxidants but less well known is that it contains a substance called theanine. Theanine is an amino acid that helps you relax and focus at the same time thus aiding your productivity. The honey also contains high levels of amino acids essential for providing the building blocks of protein the brain needs to operate at its best.

Yields: 2 Servings

Ingredients:

- 120ml water
- 1 green tea bag
- 1 tablespoon honey
- 170g blueberries
- ½ frozen banana
- 135ml soy milk

Directions:

1. Boil the half cup of water and add the tea bag. Let it steep for 3 minutes then remove the bag.
2. Place all the ingredients into the blender and blitz until smooth. Enjoy immediately.

Health benefits:

- ✓ Very high in vitamins C and B6
- ✓ High in manganese
- ✓ High in dietary fiber
- ✓ Low in sodium
- ✓ Very low in saturated fat
- ✓ Cholesterol Free!

Nutritional values per serving: Calories: 161; Total Fats: 1.5g; Cholesterol: 0mg; Sodium: 33mg; Potassium: 296mg; Carbohydrates: 36.8g; Protein: 3.2g

Brain Bomb Smoothie

Blueberries are a superfood and they are packed with antioxidants that help protect the brains cells against free radical damage. Kale is packed with iron, while mineral rich honey adds further brain cell protection. This smoothie is literally like a bomb of nutrition going off in your brain.

Yields: 2 Servings

Ingredients:

- 100g blueberries
- 135ml unsweetened almond milk
- 1 handful of kale
- 55g carrot – peeled and sliced
- ½ frozen banana
- 5 almonds – whole, unsalted
- 2 teaspoons honey

Directions:

1. Tip all the ingredients into your blender and blitz them until smooth.
2. Drink it up and wait for the explosion!

Health benefits:

- ✓ Very high in vitamins B6, C, and E
- ✓ High in vitamin A
- ✓ High in manganese
- ✓ High in calcium
- ✓ High in dietary fiber
- ✓ Low in saturated fat
- ✓ Very low in sodium
- ✓ Cholesterol Free!

Nutritional values per serving: Calories: 159; Total Fats: 3g; Cholesterol: 0mg; Sodium: 108mg; Potassium: 425mg; Carbohydrates: 29.3g; Protein: 2.7g

M.A.S.S. Smoothie

Avocadoes have a high vitamin E content, which has been known to help reduce a person's risk of contracting Alzheimer's disease. The spinach has omega-3s which supports brain functions and helps to supply your body with iron. The mass of nutrients contained in this smoothie are critical for continued brain health.

Yields: 2 Servings

Ingredients:

- ½ large mango – peeled and pitted
- ½ avocado – pitted and peeled
- 270ml soy milk
- 115g spinach
- Stevia to taste

Directions:

1. Place it all in the blender and blitz until it is all smooth.
2. Sip with a straw.
3. Be healthy!

Health benefits:

- ✓ Very high in vitamin C
- ✓ High in vitamin A
- ✓ Low in sodium
- ✓ Cholesterol Free!

Nutritional values per serving: Calories: 233; Total Fats: 12.2g; Cholesterol: 0mg; Sodium: 74mg; Potassium: 592mg; Carbohydrates: 28.7g; Protein: 5.4g

B.B. King Smoothie

The humble beet is high in fiber, beta carotene, folate, phytonutrients and natural nitrates that help increase blood flow to the brain. The more blood that enters the brain, the more oxygen there is that gets delivered, which means you can think clearly, concentrate and focus. This beet smoothie is also great for people with high blood pressure for the same reasons.

Yields: 2 Servings

Ingredients:

- 1 medium beet – peeled and chopped
- 240ml cup coconut water (or water)
- 50g blueberries
- 140g strawberries, halved
- 45g almonds – unsalted
- 100g cup ice
- 1 teaspoon fresh lime juice
- Stevia if desired

Directions:

1. Tip all the ingredients into your blender and blitz them until smooth.
2. Drink and enjoy!

Health benefits:

- ✓ Very high in vitamins B6 and A
- ✓ High in vitamin C
- ✓ High in manganese
- ✓ High in dietary fiber
- ✓ Low in sodium
- ✓ Low in saturated fat
- ✓ Cholesterol Free!

Nutritional values per serving: Calories: 189; Total Fats: 6.2g; Cholesterol: 0mg; Sodium: 162mg; Potassium: 655mg; Carbohydrates: 22g; Protein: 4.8g

Pine-Nut Smoothie

Coconut is high in manganese, fiber, very high in medium-chain triglycerides and low in natural sugars. During periods of low blood sugar, medium-chain triglycerides are converted into a source of fuel, keeping your brain functioning at a high level, so drink this smoothie for peak performance!

Yields: 2 Servings

Ingredients:

- 115g pineapple (fresh or frozen)
- 1 frozen banana
- 150ml coconut milk – unsweetened
- 120ml soy milk
- 1 tsp vanilla extract

Directions:

1. Add all the ingredients to your blender and blend until smooth.
2. Drink it all.
3. Enjoy the benefits!

Health benefits:

- ✓ Very high in vitamin C
- ✓ Very high in manganese
- ✓ Low in sodium
- ✓ Cholesterol Free!

Nutritional values per serving: Calories: 271; Total Fats: 15.8g; Cholesterol: 0mg; Sodium: 42mg; Potassium: 534mg; Carbohydrates: 31.7g; Protein: 4.8g

Pomberry Smoothie

The fiber in our diets helps to regulate blood sugar. Glucose is the brains chief energy source. Thus a regular intake of fiber is essential to keep the brain functioning optimally. This smoothie has a high fiber content and a host of other brain friendly vitamins and minerals.

Yields: 2 Servings

Ingredients:

- 2 pears, chopped
- 240ml pomegranate juice – fresh
- 130g fat free Greek yoghurt
- 5 strawberries, hulled
- 1 tablespoon honey
- 1 tablespoon chia seeds
- 100g ice

Directions:

1. Add all the ingredients to your blender and blend until smooth.
2. Pour into a glass and sip at your leisure!

Health benefits:

- ✓ Very high in vitamin C
- ✓ High in fiber
- ✓ Very low in sodium
- ✓ Cholesterol Free!

Nutritional values per serving: Calories: 304; Total Fats: 2.8g; Cholesterol: 0mg; Sodium: 69mg; Potassium: 647mg; Carbohydrates: 65.3g; Protein: 6.4g

Big D Smoothie

Big D Smoothie

Dopamine is a neurotransmitter which plays a role in pleasure, emotion, and motivation. It is easily bolstered by consuming healthy portions of protein. The soy milk and whey powder found in this smoothie are excellent sources of quality protein. The chia seeds will help keep your blood sugar steady while the espresso will help keep you focused and energized.

Yields: 2 Servings

Ingredients:

- 1 frozen banana
- 1 tablespoon chia seeds
- 270ml soy milk
- 1 teaspoon ground cinnamon
- 1 double espresso
- 30g whey powder
- Stevia to taste

Directions:

1. Place it all in the blender and blitz until it is all smooth.
2. Pour, sip and enjoy the buzz!

Health benefits:

✓ High in manganese

✓ High in dietary fiber

Nutritional values per serving: Calories: 213; Total Fats: 5.5g; Cholesterol: 23mg; Sodium: 149mg; Potassium: 478mg; Carbohydrates: 24.2g; Protein: 15.8g

Fruit Medley Smoothie

Inflammation is as serious a problem for your brain as for your body. Raspberries and strawberries are believed to have mild anti-inflammatory properties. Chia seeds are a good source of omega-3 fatty acids which is believed to be necessary for transmitting nerve signals from the brain to the whole body.

Yields: 2 Servings

Ingredients:

- 115g pomegranate juice
- ½ frozen banana
- 5 strawberries, hulled
- 55g raspberries
- 55g pineapple
- 2 tablespoons chia seeds

Directions:

1. Tip all the ingredients into your blender and blitz them until smooth.
2. Drink and enjoy!

Health benefits:

- ✓ Very high in vitamin C
- ✓ Very high in manganese
- ✓ High in dietary fiber
- ✓ Very low in sodium
- ✓ Low in saturated fat
- ✓ Cholesterol Free!

Nutritional values per serving: Calories: 133; Total Fats: 2.8g; Cholesterol: 0mg; Sodium: 5mg; Potassium: 441mg; Carbohydrates: 28.8g; Protein: 2.6g

Protein Punch Smoothies

(10g of Protein or more)

High protein diets are the hottest thing since hamburgers and everybody seems to want a slice of the action. Body builders, gym bunnies, and dieters alike are gulping down protein shakes and munching on protein bars in the hopes of gaining muscle and losing fat. This fervent level of obsession is not entirely misplaced, protein is one of the most important macronutrients needed by our body along with carbohydrates and fat. However, the difference is that the body can store fat and carbs and then draw on the reserves later when they are needed. The body does not store protein, so you need a constant supply of it to keep the body running in peak condition.

Protein is germane to a number of important body processes as well as being a component in every single cell in the body. Your hair and nails are chiefly composed of protein. You need protein to synthesize hormones, enzymes and other chemicals. Protein helps to build and repair tissues, muscles, bones, cartilage, blood and skin. Furthermore, when you digest proteins they leave behind substances called amino acids which our body needs to break down other foods that we eat. Protein also helps to keep your appetite in check thereby helping you to maintain a healthy weight.

Now you would think that the answer is to just eat protein all day, but it has been shown that quality over quantity is a better solution. Despite all the vital processes that need protein, we actually need a surprisingly small amount of protein every day for our body to function optimally. You only need between 5 and 7 ounces of protein every day to meet the body's requirements, depending on your age, sex and activity level. The trick is to get that protein from high quality sources.

Smoothies are a great way to ensure that you are getting enough protein in your diet and to ensure that it is coming from pure sources. Simply adding in one or more of these high protein, super tasty ingredients to your smoothie will help you meet your daily protein quota, so the next time you make a smoothie try adding some peanut butter, coconut milk, flax seeds, oats, seaweed, chia seeds, fat-free organic milk, almond butter, pumpkin seeds, quinoa, raw egg, plain fat-free Greek yoghurt, sunflower seeds, soy milk, kale, collard greens, spinach, avocado, walnuts, hemp seeds, or even cacao nibs.

Banana Booster Shake

This smoothie is made from all natural high protein ingredients. The almonds, soy milk and pumpkin seeds are great sources of quality protein. They also make it easy and convenient to up the protein content further by just adding more of these ingredients. The raisins are great natural sweeteners, so making the smoothie sweeter is almost guilt free. To make this a green smoothie just add ½ a cup of tightly packed spinach.

Yields: 2 Servings

Ingredients:

- 1 frozen banana
- 270ml soy milk
- ½ pear – cored
- 45g almonds
- 1 tablespoon raisins
- 1 tablespoon pumpkin seeds

Directions:

1. Pour the soy milk into your blender and then add the almonds, raisins and pumpkin seeds. Blitz until fine.
2. Add the remaining ingredients and blitz until smooth.
3. Sip and enjoy!

Health benefits:

- ✓ High in protein
- ✓ High in manganese
- ✓ Very low in sodium
- ✓ Cholesterol Free!

Nutritional values per serving: Calories 262; Total Fats: 10.1g; Cholesterol: 0mg; Sodium: 65mg; Potassium: 482mg; Carbohydrates: 31.6g; Protein: 10.6g

Mediterranean Smoothie

Fat free Greek yoghurt is the best yoghurt to use in your smoothies as it has double the protein content and less than half the salt of regular yoghurt. It is also thicker and creamier than regular yoghurt thus aiding the texture of your smoothies. Adding oil is an effective way to help round out the nutrition and provide a boost of energy! The grapes and mango give the smoothie delicious flavors and along with the spinach, a healthy dose of vitamins to go with the protein.

Yields: 2 Servings

Ingredients:

- 210ml Greek fat-free yoghurt
- 1 tablespoon of olive oil
- 1 handful of spinach
- ½ large mango – peeled, no pip
- 115g green seedless grapes
- 100g ice

Directions:

1. Throw it all in your blender and blitz until smooth and creamy.
2. Drink it immediately.
3. Enjoy!

Health benefits:

- ✓ Very high in vitamin B6
- ✓ High in vitamins A and C
- ✓ Very low in sodium
- ✓ Cholesterol Free!

Nutritional values per serving: Calories: 216; Total Fats: 8g; Cholesterol: 0mg; Sodium: 58mg; Potassium: 262mg; Carbohydrates: 25.4g; Protein: 24g

Peanut Pantaloons Smoothie

This creamy cold treat is so yummy you will forget that it is actually healthy for you! Peanuts have a serious nutritional whack. They have manganese, folate, niacin, vitamin E and most importantly a high protein content. This legume is also known to be a great source of heart protective antioxidants and mono-saturated fats.

Yields: 2 Servings

Ingredients:

- 1 frozen banana
- 270ml soy milk
- 3 tablespoons organic peanut butter
- 1 teaspoon honey
- 100g ice

Directions:

1. Place all the ingredients into the blender and blitz until smooth, creamy and delicious.
2. Enjoy!

Health benefits:

- ✓ High in protein
- ✓ Very high in B6
- ✓ High in manganese
- ✓ Cholesterol Free!

Nutritional values per serving: Calories: 270; Total Fats: 14.2g; Cholesterol: 0mg; Sodium: 173mg; Potassium: 513g; Carbohydrates: 28.7g; Protein: 11.8g

Papaya Princess Smoothie

Make tummy aches a thing of the past with this easy and quick smoothie recipe. It is loaded with ingredients that will help soothe your stomach while being high in protein to keep your body strong. Mint and ginger work together to ease an upset stomach while papaya aids digestive health. The yoghurt also delivers a helpful dose of probiotics and the lemon raises the vitamin C content.

Yields: 2 Servings

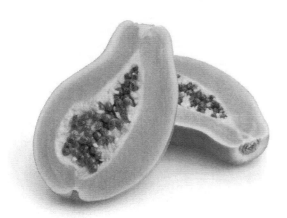

Ingredients:

- 1 papaya, seeds removed
- 130g fat free Greek yoghurt
- 60ml lemon juice
- 2 teaspoons ginger – ground
- 1 tablespoon sunflower seeds
- Sprig of mint
- 100g ice

Directions:

1. Combine all the ingredients in your blender and blend to taste.
2. Sip and enjoy!

Health benefits:

- ✓ High in protein
- ✓ Very high in vitamin A and C
- ✓ High in dietary fiber
- ✓ Low in saturated fats
- ✓ Low in sodium
- ✓ Cholesterol Free!

Nutritional values per serving: Calories: 140; Total Fats: 1.3g; Cholesterol: 0mg; Sodium: 55mg; Potassium: 421mg; Carbohydrates: 13.8g; Protein: 10.1

Nuclear Nut Smoothie

This nutty explosion is packed full of high quality protein and rich nutty flavors. This smoothie is ideal for pre-workout loading as it has a high calorie count, giving you loads of energy to get you through your training session.

Yields: 2 Servings

Ingredients:

- 270ml unsweetened almond milk
- 1 frozen banana
- 45g almonds
- 45g hazel nuts
- 45g pecan nut
- 1 ½ tablespoon raw cacao powder
- ¼ teaspoon vanilla extract
- Stevia to taste

Directions:

1. Place all the ingredients in your blender except the ice, and blitz until smooth.
2. Add the ice and blitz until smooth again. Drink and feel energized!

Health benefits:

- ✓ High in protein
- ✓ High in manganese and magnesium
- ✓ Very high in vitamin E
- ✓ Cholesterol Free!

Nutritional values per serving: Calories: 359; Total Fats: 27.1g; Cholesterol: 0mg; Sodium: 93mg; Potassium: 482mg; Carbohydrates: 22.5g; Protein: 10.2g

P.P.B. & K. Smoothie

The days of skipping breakfast are over! You can start your day with a smoothie now, containing a nutritional serving of fruits and vegetables and a high dose of protein to keep you feeling full for longer. This tasty, green high protein smoothie is a quick and convenient way to power up for whatever the day throws at you.

Yields: 2 Servings

Ingredients:

- 1 peach
- ½ frozen banana
- 115g fresh or frozen pineapple
- 1 handful of kale
- 270ml soy milk
- 3 tablespoons flaxseed – ground
- 3 tablespoons pumpkin seeds

Directions:

1. Combine all the ingredients in your blender and blend until smooth.
2. Drink up and supercharge for your day ahead!

Health benefits:

- ✓ High in protein
- ✓ Very high in vitamins A and C
- ✓ High in phosphorus and magnesium
- ✓ Very high in manganese
- ✓ Low in sodium
- ✓ Cholesterol Free!

Nutritional values per serving: Calories: 290; Total Fats: 11.5; Cholesterol: 0mg; Sodium: 76mg; Potassium: 677mg; Carbohydrates: 32.8g; Protein: 10.6g

Orange Express Smoothie

This is another great breakfast or post work-out smoothie. The protein will help with muscle repair and regeneration, while the vitamins and minerals will help energy levels and electrolyte balance. The flavors of this smoothie are also very interesting and unusual with the use of orange zest and hempseed. Guaranteed to keep the taste buds entertained.

Yields: 2 Servings

Ingredients:

- 270ml soy milk
- 180ml orange juice – freshly squeezed
- ½ banana
- 4 tablespoons hempseed – ground and shelled
- 1 teaspoon honey
- 1 teaspoon orange zest
- 100g ice

Directions:

1. Combine all the ingredients in your blender and blitz until smooth.
2. Drink it up.
3. Enjoy!

Health benefits:

- ✓ High in protein
- ✓ Very high in vitamins C and B6
- ✓ Low in sodium
- ✓ Low in saturated fat
- ✓ Cholesterol Free!

Nutritional values per serving: Calories: 237; Total Fats: 9.2g; Cholesterol: 0mg; Sodium: 66mg; Potassium: 609mg; Carbohydrates: 30g; Protein: 10.1g

Grape-berry Smoothie

Grape-berry Smoothie

Try not to eat all the grapes before you make your smoothie! The succulence of the juicy, plump grapes is hard enough to resist, but knowing what a great source of powerful antioxidants, potassium, magnesium and vitamin C they are makes it even harder. This vitamin and protein packed smoothie is a great all-rounder. Great for active people as well as people needing a health boost.

Yields: 2 Servings

Ingredients:

- 250g seedless grapes
- 50g blueberries
- 3 tablespoon chia seeds
- 3 tablespoon pumpkin seeds
- 270ml fat free Greek yoghurt
- 100g ice

Directions:

1. Place everything into your blender and blitz until it is completely smooth.
2. Sip slowly and enjoy!

Health benefits:

- ✓ High in protein
- ✓ Very high in vitamin B
- ✓ Very high in manganese
- ✓ High in vitamin C
- ✓ High in magnesium
- ✓ High in dietary fiber
- ✓ Low in sodium
- ✓ Cholesterol Free!

Nutritional values per serving: Calories: 208; Total Fats: 10.2g; Cholesterol: 0mg; Sodium: 41mg; Potassium: 339mg; Carbohydrates: 26.6g; Protein: 10.7g

Oats and Banana Smoothie

The star of this 'breakfast cereal' smoothie is the banana. Whilst being a high protein smoothie it is the potassium from the banana which protects the heart muscles and promotes calcium absorption. This make it an ideal pre-workout smoothie as it will give you a healthy long release of energy as well as preventing muscle cramps.

Yields: 2 Servings

Ingredients:

- 4 tablespoons rolled oats
- 1 frozen banana
- 270ml soy milk
- 1 teaspoon honey
- ¼ teaspoon cinnamon

Directions:

1. Place all the ingredients into your blender and blitz until completely smooth.
2. Drink!
3. Enjoy!

Health benefits:

- ✓ Cholesterol free!
- ✓ High in protein
- ✓ Low in saturated fat
- ✓ High in manganese
- ✓ Low in sodium

Nutritional values per serving: Calories: 169; Total Fats: 2.8g; Cholesterol: 0mg; Sodium: 66mg Potassium: 396mg; Carbohydrates: 31.2g; Protein: 11.9g

The Whey Smoothie

People who train with heavier weights or for longer than most need a higher protein intake. This can make the difference between waking up with sore muscles the next day and feeling stronger. This smoothie contains the protein your body needs to rejuvenate and recover effectively, whilst maximizing your strength.

Yields: 2 Servings

Ingredients:

- 30g whey powder
- 1 pear
- 5 strawberries
- 375g soy milk
- 3 tablespoons fat free Greek yoghurt
- 2 tablespoons chia seeds
- ¼ teaspoon vanilla extract

Directions:

1. Pour the soy milk and the protein powder into your blender and blitz until completely mixed.
2. Add the remaining ingredients and blitz again until smooth.
3. Drink and feel stronger!

Health benefits:

- ✓ Very high in protein
- ✓ Very high in B6
- ✓ High in dietary fiver
- ✓ Very high in manganese

Nutritional values per serving: Calories: 330; Total Fats: 16.2g; Cholesterol: 23mg; Sodium: 197mg; Potassium: 501mg; Carbohydrates: 26.7; Protein: 22g

Heart Healthy Smoothies

The heart is the most important organ in the body. Most people consider the brain to be the most important organ in the body as it is the seat of all our higher order functions, but technically you are still classed as alive when your brain is dead and this is solely because your heart remains beating. Once the heart beats for the last time everything else dies too. The heart has the biggest role of responsibility in the body as everything else depends on it. It is therefore vital that we take every precaution to protect the heart and keep it functioning optimally.

Heart health is becoming an increasing cause for concern with the sudden rise in incidence of heart disease and chronic heart conditions. At the root of this wide spread degeneration in overall heart health is what we put into our bodies. Our food is too fatty, too rich, and packed full of all the wrong things – it's that simple! If we want to take care of our heart we need to clean up our diets. Now while we might all know that eating certain foods are better for us, it is often difficult to change eating habits that have become entrenched over many years. With this in mind there are a number of small steps you can take to put you on the road to a healthy heart and fortunately most of these are able to be incorporated into your new smoothie lifestyle.

Fruits and vegetables are your one way ticket to a healthy heart because they are loaded with vitamins and minerals that specifically fight off cardiovascular disease. There is no easier way to get enough fruit and vegetables into your daily diet than through smoothies. Limit the inclusion of unhealthy fats and cholesterol in your diet. They add no value to your body and only succeed in clogging up your arteries and paving the way for a heart attack. Make sure you limit the amount of sodium you consume. Sodium leads to high blood pressure which puts strain on your heart by making it pump faster than it is supposed to. Limiting processed foods will go a long way to reduce sodium intake as these are typically loaded with hidden salts that you are probably not even aware you are consuming. Flavor your food and your smoothies with a selection of fresh herbs and spices instead. These small changes to your daily diet will see you reaping the benefits of good heart health for years to come.

Prevention is far better (and easier) than cure! Rather take the necessary steps to keep your heart healthy than try to reverse damage already done to your heart. A very good way to prevent the development of heart problems is to include one or more of the following heart healthy ingredients into your smoothies. Oats and flax seeds are excellent whole grains that offer protection to the heart. Choose low fat milks and yoghurts over full fat options and soy products are also excellent for a healthy heart. Other superb additions to your smoothies include, all nuts (but especially almonds and walnuts), tofu, soy milk, berries (especially blueberries), carrots, spinach, okra, broccoli, oranges, bananas, cantaloupe, papaya, dark chocolate chips, green tea, raisins, flaxseed oil, raw cacao powder, apples and pomegranates.

The Italian Stallion Smoothie

This heart healthy smoothie is bursting with a variety of healthy vitamins and minerals. All of which are essential in maintaining a healthy body and a healthy heart. It has no cholesterol and the celery contains a phytochemical called phthalide. Phthalide relaxes and smooth's the muscles in the arteries thereby lowering blood pressure. Enjoy this deliciously savory smoothie as a meal or a snack.

Yields: 2 Servings

Ingredients:

- 2 large tomatoes
- 1 red bell pepper
- 2 cloves garlic
- 2 celery stalks
- 55g carrots
- 70g watercress
- 115g spinach
- 120ml water

Directions:

1. Throw all the ingredients into your blender and blend thoroughly.
2. Sip slowly and enjoy!

Health benefits:

- ✓ Very high in vitamins A, B6 and C
- ✓ Very high in potassium
- ✓ High in thiamin
- ✓ High in dietary fiber
- ✓ Very low in saturated fat
- ✓ Cholesterol Free!

Nutritional values per serving: Calories: 55; Total Fats: 0.4g; Cholesterol: 0mg; Sodium: 366mg; Potassium: 562mg; Carbohydrates: 11.9g; Protein: 2.4g

Blue Avo Smoothie

Blueberries are loaded with disease fighting phytochemicals and antioxidants. Avocadoes are rich in monosaturated fatty acids, which many studies have shown to help lower our risk of heart disease. The folic acid and B6 found in this smoothie also provide helpful heart support.

Yields: 2 Servings

Ingredients:

- 100g blueberries
- 1 avocado, pitted and peeled
- 240ml coconut water
- 60ml lemon juice
- 100g ice cubes

Directions:

1. Combine all the ingredients in your blender and blitz until smooth.
2. Drink.
3. Delicious!

Health benefits:

- ✓ Very high in vitamins C and B6
- ✓ High in dietary fiber
- ✓ Very low in sodium
- ✓ Cholesterol Free!

Nutritional values per serving: Calories: 277; Total Fats: 20.3g; Cholesterol: 0mg; Sodium: 140mg; Potassium: 882mg; Carbohydrates: 24.2g; Protein: 3.6g

The Calpot Smoothie

The yoghurt and milk's potassium and calcium combine in helping to lower blood pressure as well as helping with weight control, by making you feel satisfied and full for longer. The flavanols that are extracted from the cacao bean help in promoting a healthy circulatory system. Studies show that almonds are very good for reducing LDL, the bad cholesterol, and raising the levels of HDL, the good cholesterol.

Yields: 2 Servings

Ingredients:

- 130g Greek yoghurt
- 115g soy milk
- ½ frozen banana
- 50g raspberries
- 2 tablespoons raisins
- 1 tablespoon almond butter
- 1 teaspoon dark cacao powder

Directions:

1. Introduce all the ingredients to the blender and blitz until smooth.
2. Drink. An absolute treat for your taste buds!

Health benefits:

- ✓ Very high in phosphorus
- ✓ High in vitamin C
- ✓ Low in sodium
- ✓ Low in saturated fat
- ✓ Very low in cholesterol

Nutritional values per serving: Calories: 194; Total Fats: 5.1g; Cholesterol: 1mg; Sodium: 34mg; Potassium: 376mg; Carbohydrates: 26.5g; Protein: 9.8g

The A.C. Smoothie

Acai berries are super-loaded with antioxidants and have also been shown in some studies to increase the levels of good cholesterol and help in the prevention of atherosclerosis. Chia seeds are also packed full of antioxidants. Besides all their well-known positive properties, they have also been shown to help lower blood pressure. They also have significant levels of omega-3 fatty acids which are beneficial to your cardiovascular health.

Yields: 1 Serving

Ingredients:

- 115g acai berries
- 2 tablespoons chia seeds
- 270ml unsweetened almond milk
- 1 tablespoon honey
- 100g ice

Directions:

1. Add the acai berries and the soy milk to your blender and blitz until the berries are thoroughly chopped.
2. Add the remaining ingredients and blitz until smooth.
3. Devour and feel the benefits!

Health benefits:

- ✓ High in vitamin E
- ✓ High in manganese
- ✓ High in calcium
- ✓ Low in saturated fat
- ✓ Cholesterol Free!

Nutritional values per serving: Calories: 397; Total Fats: 11.9g; Cholesterol: 0mg; Sodium: 388mg; Potassium: 386mg; Carbohydrates: 20g; Protein: 51.5g

The Hemp Hemp Hooray Smoothie

Hemp seeds contain an almost perfect balance of omega-3 to omega-6 essential fatty acids. This is vitally important to heart health and the revitalization of cardiovascular function and circulation. Strawberries are a perfect match for heart health because they are naturally fat, sodium, and cholesterol-free.

Yields: 2 Servings

Ingredients:

- 4 tablespoons of hemp seeds
- 270ml unsweetened almond milk
- 135ml fat free Greek yoghurt
- 7 large strawberries
- 140g raspberries
- ½ teaspoon vanilla extract
- 100g ice

Directions:

1. Place all the ingredients in your blender and blitz until smooth.
2. Drink and be healthy!

Health benefits:

- ✓ Very high in vitamin C
- ✓ Very high in manganese
- ✓ Low in saturated fat
- ✓ Very high in dietary fiber
- ✓ Cholesterol Free!

Nutritional values per serving: Calories: 293; Total Fats: 6.4g; Cholesterol: 0mg; Sodium: 262mg; Potassium: 982mg; Carbohydrates: 59.5g; Protein: 16.4g

Happy Heart Smoothie

Happy Heart Smoothie

Orange juice contains an antioxidant called hesperidin which improves blood vessel function and also lowers a person risk of heart disease. Papayas are thought to be helpful in the prevention of atherosclerosis because of their significant vitamin E and C content. Carrots also have good levels of antioxidants which are known to protect the cardiovascular system.

Yields: 2 Servings

Ingredients:

- ½ papaya – chopped
- ½ frozen banana
- ½ whole carrot
- 120ml orange juice – freshly squeezed
- 30g frozen blueberries
- 100g red grapes

Directions:

1. Throw all the ingredients into your blender and blitz until smooth.
2. Drink this yummy blend chilled.
3. Enjoy!

Health benefits:

- ✓ Very high in vitamins C, B6 and A
- ✓ High in potassium
- ✓ High in dietary fiber
- ✓ Low in sodium
- ✓ Very low in saturated fat
- ✓ Cholesterol Free!

Nutritional values per serving: Calories: 120; Total Fats: 0.4g; Cholesterol: 0mg; Sodium: 20mg; Potassium: 474mg; Carbohydrates: 29.3g; Protein: 1.6g

The Sweet-Tart Smoothie

This smoothie brings together two super fruits, pomegranate and blueberries in one potent, both sweet and tart smoothie. Both have very high concentrations of antioxidants that help in protecting your blood vessels and heart from disease. The berries are also high in fiber which helps to lower cholesterol.

Yields: 1 Serving

Ingredients:

- 80g blueberries
- 120ml pomegranate juice
- 130g Greek fat free yoghurt
- ½ teaspoon lemon zest
- 1 teaspoon lemon juice
- Stevia to taste
- 100g ice

Directions:

1. Place all the ingredients in your blender and blitz until smooth.
2. Serve immediately.
3. YUM!

Health benefits:

- ✓ Very high in vitamins C and B6
- ✓ High in manganese
- ✓ High in dietary fiber
- ✓ Very low in sodium
- ✓ Very low in saturated fat
- ✓ Cholesterol Free!

Nutritional values per serving: Calories: 135; Total Fats: 0.6g; Cholesterol: 0mg; Sodium: 9mg; Potassium: 95mg; Carbohydrates: 20.9g; Protein: 8.5g

Green Apple Smoothie

We all know the saying "an apple a day keeps the doctor away" - well the more research that is done into the health benefits of this popular fruit, the more it seems to be true! Apples have been found to contain compounds that delay the breakdown of LDL, the bad cholesterol, thus allowing our bodies to eliminate it before it enters our systems.

Yields: 2 Servings

Ingredients:

- 1 green apple – cored, sliced and skin on
- ½ large mango, chopped
- 1 small handful of spinach
- 120ml soy milk
- 1 teaspoon ginger
- Stevia to taste

Directions:

1. Toss all the ingredients into your blender and blitz until smooth.
2. Drink it up.
3. Enjoy!

Health benefits:

- ✓ Very high in vitamins C and B6
- ✓ High in vitamin A
- ✓ High in dietary fiber
- ✓ Very low in sodium
- ✓ Very low in saturated fat
- ✓ Cholesterol Free!

Nutritional values per serving: Calories: 93; Total Fats: 0.2g; Cholesterol: 0mg; Sodium: 7mg; Potassium: 216mg; Carbohydrates: 23.4g; Protein: 0.4g

Humming Heart Smoothie

Studies have shown that, although honey is made up mostly of sugar which is traditionally considered bad for your heart health, honey affects us differently by actually lowering cholesterol levels in the study groups that were investigated. That combined with its multitude of vitamins, minerals and amino acids makes it a beneficial addition to any heart healthy smoothie.

Yields: 2 Servings

Ingredients:

- 2 tablespoons honey
- 60ml orange juice
- 120ml soy milk
- u½ frozen banana
- ½ avocado – pitted and peeled

Directions:

1. Combine all the ingredients in your blender and blitz until smooth.
2. Drink it all.
3. It's amazing!

Health benefits:

- ✓ Very high in vitamins C and B6
- ✓ Low in sodium
- ✓ Very low cholesterol

Nutritional values per serving: Calories: 240; Total Fats: 10.9g; Cholesterol: 0mg; Sodium: 39mg; Potassium: 496mg; Carbohydrates: 35.2g; Protein: 3.3g

Banana Boom-Boom Smoothie

Why not close this book with an all-time favorite? This easy to make simple smoothie is great for heart health. The banana is loaded with potassium which helps lower blood pressure and also helps to regulate the fluid salt balance in your cells. The blueberries and kale are packed with antioxidants and fiber, both of which help combat heart disease and help in the neutralization of free radicals. Bottoms up!

Yields: 2 Servings

Ingredients:

- 1 frozen banana
- 1 handful of kale
- 100g blueberries
- 270ml unsweetened almond milk
- Stevia to taste

Directions:

1. Throw all the ingredients into your blender and blitz till smooth.
2. Drink and enjoy!

Health benefits:

- ✓ Very high in vitamins C, B6 and A
- ✓ High in potassium
- ✓ High in dietary fiber
- ✓ Very low in sodium
- ✓ Very low in saturated fat
- ✓ Cholesterol Free!

Nutritional values per serving: Calories: 129; Total Fats: 0.1g; Cholesterol: 0mg; Sodium: 10mg; Potassium: 513mg; Carbohydrates: 32.6g; Protein: 1.9g

Conclusion

And that's a wrap ☺. This book of delicious smoothies covers all the major aspects of good health that will start you on your journey to wellness. So blend, sip and enjoy feeling ALL the phenomenal health benefits that await you.

This book is just the tip of the ice berg regarding just how much you can achieve through smoothies. As you become a more seasoned smoothie expert, you can start making your own smoothie recipes based on your experiences and personal preferences. Literally a whole world awaits you, the only obstacle is your own creativity.

So embrace your creativity, channel your inner smoothie chef, mix in a heaping spoonful of enthusiasm and remember to have fun! Smoothies for the most part are incredibly forgiving, but should you have a culinary disaster, simply block your nose, chug it down, chalk it up to experience and start again tomorrow! The whole point of smoothies is to enjoy good health, not to feel enslaved by yet another set of dietary restrictions. So love what you do and laugh a lot – that's the recipe for smoothie success!

And finally let's raise our smoothie glasses and toast "To you and your good health"

Cheers!

Diana Clayton

Recommendations

... More Low Calorie Goodness!

Hungry for more? Pick up the latest editions of low calorie books from Diana. Just search Amazon for "Diana Clayton" and discover even *more* incredible recipes, all while shedding some pounds. Diana's low calorie cookbook collection includes ....

Amazon Bestseller!

Slow Cooker Recipe Book:
Dieter's Paradise:

Heavenly Slow Cooker Recipes
from All Around the World,

All Under 500 Calories!

Amazon Feature!

5:2 Diet Recipe Book, All Under 300 Calories

Healthy & Filling 5:2 Fast Diet Recipes to Lose Weight and Enhance your Health

Fan Favorite!

5:2 Fast Diet Recipe Book: Meals for One!

Amazing Single Serving 5:2 Fast Diet Recipes to Lose More Weight with Intermittent Fasting

And much more to come . . .
Enjoy!

Index

References are to page numbers.

114

Printed in Great Britain
by Amazon.co.uk, Ltd.,
Marston Gate.